Read All About It

My year of falling in love with literature again

PAUL CUDDIHY

Contents

'No matter how busy you may think you are, you must find time for reading, or surrender yourself to self-chosen ignorance.'
Confucius

'Every night I have to read a book so that my mind will stop thinking about things that I stress about.'
Britney Spears

Introduction

'I have never been able to resist a book about books.'
Anne Fadiman

'What age was I when I learned to read?' I want my mum to tell me I was three or four-years-old, confirming, even all these decades later, that I was a prodigiously talented child and destined for a life in letters. I've always believed that I could read even before I started school, taught by my mum, who was a primary school teacher herself. Her answer, after a few moments' consideration, therefore, comes as a slight disappointment.

'I think you were five or six. You didn't read before you went to school because I didn't want to teach you before you started. You would have learned in primary one and by primary two you would have been a very good reader.'

It shouldn't really matter now, over forty years later, that my delusions of genius are just that. In truth, I don't remember a time when I couldn't read, and regardless of what age I learned, it has remained one of the greatest gifts ever bestowed on me. I apologise if that sounds somewhat grandiose, but it is true. The sentiments also fit in nicely with this book and what I'm attempting to do with it. I wanted to, as the title suggests, fall in love with literature again, and over the course of 2013, my aim was to read more books. I had grown lazy in my reading habits over a period of time, blaming work, children, tiredness and television amongst other things for having done little to tackle my ever-expanding collection of books.

I wonder how many books I have actually read since those early days of primary school and the *'Peter and Jane'* series of books which were used to teach children in Scottish schools back in the early 1970s. I start to think about childhood memories of reading, though the most vivid ones remain wrapped up with corporal punishment that was also part and parcel of school life in Scotland back then.

Those of you of a similar vintage will remember the SRA (Science Research Associates) reading programme that was taught in schools, with different colour coding being used to determine the level of reading competency of each child. The aim was obviously to encourage reading but also to challenge pupils to improve and, therefore, move up the colour chart; I think silver was the top one, but I could be wrong. Someone with a better memory than mine, and that could be just about anyone, can correct me if necessary. One afternoon during the weekly 'SRA time' five of us slipped *Commando* comic books inside our SRA books and read tales of derring-do against Fritz and the rest of those dastardly Nazis. We would have got away with it, too, if it wasn't for the fact one boy, whose name has been withheld to protect the idiocy, was sitting with his back to the teacher, who spied the illicit reading material. My comrade quickly buckled under interrogation and revealed his co-conspirators. In short, he 'grassed' the rest of us up and we were all belted for that transgression.

Later that same year – it was primary seven – I fell foul of our teacher again. Friday afternoon was designated 'story time', and the teacher would read to us for the last hour of the day. The book she'd chosen was *Master of Morgana* by Allan Campbell McLean, a wonderful adventure story set on the Scottish island of Skye. It was thrilling, exciting, dangerous and utterly captivating. After three weeks, I couldn't wait another seven days for the next instalment, so straight after school on the Friday I headed to the local library and borrowed the book, spending the whole weekend reading it. When I returned to school on Monday morning, not only did I boast about finishing the book, I foolishly revealed what happened in it to the rest of my classmates. When the teacher found out, I was hauled to the front of the class and belted again.

For years afterwards, I remained appalled that I had actually been punished for showing some initiative and reading in my own time. If anything was ever likely to put me off reading, then it was this incident. Of course, with age comes wisdom (hopefully) and I now realise that I was punished for being a smart-arse and ruining the book for everyone else. It was a salutary lesson, since I will endeavour, in writing about any particular book on the following pages, not to reveal all lest it spoil your own reading experiences.

Primary school punishments were always unlikely to stop me reading, though teenage angst and apathy could easily have done so. It was a problem when I was at school and it remains so to this day – how do you get teenagers, and boys in particular, to read? My suggestion, while not solving the issue, might help ... give them something to read that they might enjoy. I apologise to any English teacher reading this because I know it sounds flippant, and with a teenage son who does not read books at all, I know how difficult it is, but I think more care in the subject matter would help, and that's advice equally applicable to parents and teachers.

I just remember my own experience of secondary school and our fifth-year Higher English class. While the girls were given D.H. Lawrence's *Sons and Lovers* to study, the boys were handed *Catch 22* by Joseph Heller. It was an inspired choice by our teacher, Peter McGhee, and a class of fifteen and sixteen-year-old boys were suddenly engrossed in a book that was, first of all, hilarious and salacious, but one that, upon closer study, was also profoundly moving. It was still the funny bits that got us at that age.

I love that book, and the experience of that class, and it remains one of my fondest memories from just over five years spent at Turnbull High School, so much so that I still retain the copy I was given back in 1982. Technically, I suppose you could call that stealing, but is there not some sort of statute of limitations when it comes to these things? I'd also like to meet Peter McGhee again and shake his hand, maybe buy him a pint, and tell him that I think he probably helped to make lifetime readers of all the boys who were in that class.

If my love of books was cemented by *Catch 22*, which I actually read again last year and enjoyed just as much, then my love of writing was also in full flow by then, with endless poems churned out in the privacy of my bedroom. I still have many of them in my possession. Not surprisingly, they're not very good. This is from a poem circa 1984 entitled *Waiting for the Train.*

Every morning in the pouring rain,
She's always waiting for the train;
And I've noticed her just standing there.

Every morning in the summer sun,
She's waiting there with everyone,
And I've noticed her just standing there.

If only she knew; if only I could tell her.
If only she was mine, then I'd feel a whole lot better;
And she'd be waiting for the train,
Always sheltered from the rain,
And I'd be happy, and so would she,
But for just now I can only dream.

The poem continues in a similar vein – I will spare you any more pain – but two things immediately spring to mind on reading it again after all these years. One is that I have no recollection of who the mystery girl is that I was writing about and, two, even if I had declared any romantic intentions at the time, she'd have probably jumped under that train if she read my poem.

In much the same way that I have no pre-reading memory, the same is true about writing. It's as if, from the moment the words on a page became clear to me, then I wanted to fill blank pages with my own words. That began with stories which were pastiches of the *Roy of the Rovers'* comics I read at

4

the time, using the same characters to create my own work. I would show my efforts to my mum or dad, who would offer words of praise and encouragement, regardless of the quality. I suspect they weren't very good. I always wish my parents had kept these stories. It would have been interesting to look back on them and see if I could detect any writing 'talent' at that young age – as opposed to any writing 'talent' now, I hear you whisper cruelly. It might also have proved to be a nice little nest-egg for them on the off-chance that I ever do manage to become a famous writer, in which case they could immediately put the stories up for sale on eBay.

That encouragement was, of course, vital, in making me continue to put pen to paper and believe – I still do – that I have something to say which some people might like to read. I've tried to do the same thing with my three children, though with varying degrees of success, certainly in terms of their love of reading.

As I've grown older, and certainly in recent years, I've found that my own love of reading has been equalled, or even surpassed, by my love of buying books. It's a habit, a hobby, an obsession or a sickness, depending on your point of view and also which member of my circle of friends and family you choose to ask. I'll save you the bother of asking my wife, Karen, and tell you she believes it's a sickness.

With each book that I've bought there has been an increase in the guilt I feel at not reading enough. The motivation for this project, therefore, is to try and assuage that guilt. The idea actually came from one of my daughters, Rebecca, who in 2012, had to keep a reading diary as one of her assignments for her English class at university. It involved reading a number of different things – a novel, a short-story, a play and a poem – and it was from this that the germ of an idea began to take root in my mind. My original aim was simply to try and read more books in 2013, and just keep a note of them so that I could remember everything I read. That it has now become an Appendix in this book tells you that my initial idea has expanded somewhat.

In as much as it is possible to love inanimate objects, I do love books, and this literary journey throughout 2013 has only served to strengthen that love. I also hope, in committing my experiences to the page that you too, like Anne Fadiman, are not able to resist a book about books.

You Say You Want A Resolution

'I love the smell of book ink in the morning.'
Umberto Eco

The last song we sing at our Christmas night party is Matt McGinn's *The Wee Kirkcudbright Centipede,* at about six o'clock on Boxing Day morning. Apart from the fact that it's probably my favourite song ever, by this stage of proceedings I can't really focus on any of the words on the song sheets I brought with me, and so have resorted to playing tunes on the guitar from memory. It's a simple four-chord song and I know all the words, ingrained in my head and my heart from childhood, so it's a perfect choice. Everyone else at the party is fairly drunk as well, so no-one will even notice if I mess up the song.

Boxing Day morning comes and goes without me playing any part in it. I finally surface around three o'clock in the afternoon. Unfortunately, the local *Greggs* isn't opened for my usual hangover cure of a fudge doughnut and a chocolate doughnut, washed down with Diet Irn Bru. It's only 'diet' because I prefer the taste rather than any health or weight-conscious decision on my part.

For reasons that remain unclear to me – it may well be that I'm still half-drunk – I gravitate to the dining room where all my books reside. Doesn't everyone have a library in their dining room, or is it just those of us living in stately homes? Actually, I don't live in a stately home, but a three-bedroom semi-detached house in Bishopbriggs, a town situated about five miles from Glasgow. About four years ago Karen, fed up with the cupboard in our bedroom bursting at the seams with books, suggested building shelves along the length of one of the walls in the dining room. There were two caveats to that suggestion; the first was hers, that there would

7

be sliding 'wardrobe' doors to hide the books from sight. The second was my own – that I didn't have to put the shelves up since I am the least handy man I know. Instead, my father-in-law got out his tools and assembled a new home for my books.

Most of the shelves were quickly filled, and they have continued to welcome new arrivals in the intervening years. As I push open the 'wardrobe' doors on Boxing Day, it seems like the voices of a million characters all shout at once 'Read me!' 'Read me!' 'Read me!'

I have lots of books. Hundreds. Thousands. I don't actually know how many. I'm afraid to count them in case the revelation will lead to pressure for a clear-out or a ban imposed on any new acquisitions. Occasionally, I have resolved not to buy any more until I've made a serious dent in the ones I've already got, but then I'll spot a book in Waterstone's or in a charity shop, online or even in the supermarket, and as if by magic it will appear on my shelves, just one more to add to the pile of 'still be read' tomes. I've also realised that I will never read all the books that I own, even if I live to be one hundred. By then, I'll be lucky if I can read my congratulatory card from the Queen, or the King, or whoever's on the throne in 2066. It's a slightly depressing thought, which I take to be a sign that I'm getting old rather than an acceptance that I have too many books.

Why, on this of all days, have I decided to start reading again? The truth is, I don't know. The shelves of unread books always make me feel guilty whenever I look at them, so I don't know what makes Boxing Day so different from any other day. It's not that I haven't been reading at all, but as someone who professes to love books, and who aspires to be a great novelist – for great, I mean 'best-selling', because I actually dream of becoming Scotland's answer to Dan Brown – I have been neglecting one of the essentials tools of the trade. A writer who doesn't read is like a singer who doesn't listen to music or a plumber who doesn't like flushing the toilet. Okay, so that's maybe not such an appropriate example, but you know what I mean. Stephen King, who knows a thing or two about writing, gives this piece of advice:

'If you want to be a writer, you must do two things above all others: read a lot and write a lot.'

From the moment I learned to read, in the dim and distant past of the early 1970s, I fell in love with books and as well as wanting to keep reading, it made me want to write my own books. That it only took me about another forty years to finally achieve that ambition is a story for another day.

I knew 2012 had been a bit of a wash-out as far as reading was concerned. I had managed to publish my third novel, *Land Beyond The Wave*, the final part of what I like to call my 'Costello trilogy' following on from *Saints and Sinners* and *The Hunted* – available from all good book shops and some rubbish ones too – but while I basked in the 'Ready Brek' glow of that achievement, I wasn't doing enough of what Mr. King was advising. True, the two weeks of my summer holiday saw my reading output restored to healthy levels aided, for the first time, by a Kindle which I'd purchased specifically for the trip, but that enthusiasm for the written word soon dissipated. Where before I could sit for hours, albeit in the sunshine, and read, as soon as I returned to a grey and gloomy Glasgow – and that's the summer weather, folks – I quickly returned to my previous bad ways.

So 2013 is going to be different. I decide this with five days of the old year still remaining. I'm not waiting for a Hogmanay hangover to prompt any resolutions before tackling my ever-increasing collection of books. No, there's no time like the present, and so I begin going through the shelves, selecting any books which catch my eye. Before too long, I have a dozen to put on a newly-created 'Books To Read' shelf. My reasons for choosing a particular book, I quickly realise, are completely arbitrary. It might be because it's something I've been meaning to read for ages, or one that I feel I should read because it's worthy or has perceived literary merit. It could be that it's the cover which attracts my attention or the synopsis on the back, the same reasons that persuaded me to purchase it in the first place. I keep picking up books and thinking, 'I don't remember even buying this.'

Having resolved to make 2013 a year of reading, I figure that, if nothing else, it will make me feel better about myself, because, to paraphrase the words of the classic 1970s children's TV show, I've switched off my television set and am going to do something less boring instead. I presume it will also, in my conceit, make me think I am better than everyone else who appears to have consigned books to history and embraced digital TV, Sky+, reality TV shows and the depressing banality of social media. Okay, so I love Sky+ and I still watch a lot of telly, and I use social media and I've even watched the odd reality show here and there. The truth is that I'm no better or worse than anyone else.

Still, I do believe that reading is an infinitely more worthwhile pastime than any of the above-mentioned 'activities', and it does give me a fighting chance of retaining a basic knowledge of grammar, spelling and punctuation, all of which are being systematically destroyed by emails, text messages, Twitter and Facebook. Yes, you might spot the odd mistake here and there in what I've written, which you are free to inform me about in a suitably gloating email, but remember, if you sign off your correspondence with 'LOL' or any similar twenty-first century acronym, then we won't be friends any more. It's as simple as that. Don't say I didn't warn you!

It might be worth pointing out at this early stage of our journey that I mostly read works of fiction. That's just a personal choice. You will find the occasional non-fiction tome sneaking in over the year, but I'm basically a man who likes a good novel.

The first book I decide to tackle is *Diamonds Are Forever* by Ian Fleming. It's not that I have a burning desire to read a James Bond novel, but I had read *Casino Royale* on holiday the previous summer and enjoyed it, so I'm fairly confident that it will be, at the very least, a pleasant and painless reading experience to ease me back in. It is pleasant enough, and painless too, although the story is nowhere near as good as *Casino Royale*, which contains a brilliant last line when Bond, on the telephone to M, says of his double-crossing girlfriend, 'The bitch is dead now.'

Having succeeded where Blofeld and other baddies had failed in quickly dispensing with Mr Bond, I move on to *Scoop* by Evelyn Waugh, billed as 'the great Fleet Street novel'. It is funny, if a little dated, which is not surprising given that it was written in 1938. The language gives it away, and some of it does jar with twenty-first century sensibilities, particularly in relation to race. However, it's an enjoyable read which tells the story of William Boot, a young man who contributes 'nature notes' to the *Daily Beast* newspaper. Mistaken for a famous author of the same name, he is subsequently sent to cover a war in the fictional African Republic of Ishmaelia where he inadvertently manages to stumble upon a 'scoop' for the newspaper.

I feel better after finishing it, like it's a book I should, as a journalist as much as anything else, have read. Indeed, while sitting in the press room at a football stadium in Edinburgh, a couple of fellow journalists comment on the choice of book, while one of them promises to lend me Michael Freyn's novel about journalism, *Towards The End Of The Morning*, which he thinks I might enjoy. I won't name names, although anyone familiar with the Scottish football media can make an educated case as to their identities, given that most of the press pack are not what you would consider literary gentlemen, or indeed, in a few cases, literate gentlemen. I might be doing them a disservice but I doubt it.

I bring in the New Year with *Scoop* – not literally, or literary, I hasten to add, since I'm at another party, my acoustic guitar at the ready for festivities that go on almost as long as the previous week's Christmas ones had. Within a couple of days, I've finished that novel too, and am already on to No.3 – *We Need To Talk About Kevin* by Lionel Shriver.

It is at this point that I read an article in the *The Daily Telegraph* which, while not changing my life, certainly re-affirms what I've decided to do. Entitled 'The Half Hour That Changed My Life', the article by novelist David Nicholls describes how he'd spent the previous twelve months trying to get back into the habit of reading. Great minds think alike, eh? He got up early in the morning and would read for half an hour every day before the rest of his household wakened or the demands of work became incessant. It was habit-forming, and he explained how easy it was, with just thirty minutes set aside each day, to work his way through a whole raft of books. Nicholls explains:

Just half an hour a day can change your life. It's the sort of dubious claim you find in the back of a magazine, and I'm aware of a zealot's shrillness in all of this. I know that for every reader who has lost the habit or can't find the time, there are people who've never enjoyed reading and question the value of literature, either as entertainment or education, or believe that a love of books, and of fiction in particular, is sentimental or frivolous. Given an extra half-hour a day, I know that some people would much prefer to be jogging or bantering on social networks or simply sleeping some more. No one reaches the end of their life and wishes they'd spent more time on Twitter is a claim I've heard before, but perhaps that won't always be the case.

But to allow the zealot his voice again, think of what you might be missing by not finding the time to read. Allowing for a steady pace of a page a minute, you could easily take in a short story by Chekhov or Raymond Carver or Richard Yates every morning of next week.'

The article feels like a vindication of my reading resolution, while I can vouch for the quality of Richard Yates' short stories. His collection, *Eleven Kinds of Loneliness*, is an example of American short-story writing at its very best, as is Raymond Carver's book, *Cathedral*. The article also gives me one or two hints for my own reading habits. I'm generally an early riser anyway, but now, instead of switching on the TV and staring at the 24-hour rolling news or sports channel, or catching up with whatever is on the Sky+ box, I sit for an hour or so in blissful silence, just one man and his book.

It also helps that *We Need To Talk About Kevin* is brilliant. I can't put it down. Shriver's novel tells the story of a mother trying to come to terms with the fact her son is responsible for a killing spree in an American school, and through a series of letters to her estranged husband she reflects on their relationship, how they brought up their son and what responsibility they have for his devastating actions. The book tackles issues of nature versus nurture, violence in western culture and the ready availability of weapons in American society, and is told so brilliantly that there is a need to share the book with others and discuss it with anyone who has read it. I can understand why Shriver's novel is a favourite with reading groups.

Not wanting to lose any momentum, I quickly move on to my next book – *The Plot Against America* by Philip Roth. I like the premise – what if Charles Lindbergh had won the 1940 American presidential election, signed a peace pact with Nazi Germany and then, slowly and insidiously, started to turn America against its Jewish population? The story is told primarily through the eyes of a young Jewish boy in New York, and for three-quarters of the book, it is a captivating story. Then it seems to run out of steam and the ending, to me, feels rushed, as if Roth has lost interest and just wants to get the book finished. It's not an entirely satisfactory conclusion, though the book gets an overall thumbs-up. I have another couple of Roth novels, including the modestly-titled *The Great American Novel*, but reading *The Plot Against America* hasn't made me want to push everything else to one side and devour Roth's canon of work.

By the tenth day of January, I'm on to book No.5 and that's probably as much as I'd read in the three months leading up to Christmas. After a couple of American-based novels, I decide to get a bit closer to home and so opt for William McIlvanney's *Laidlaw*. I feel disappointed in myself as a reader, a writer, a Scot and a Glaswegian that I've never read any of McIlvanney's books. I could try and justify it in one of my general rants about the fact Scottish literature is not taught as widely in our schools as it should be, and there is a lack of awareness of such books. I actually don't know if that's true any more. It was in my day, but it's been a long time since I've been inside a classroom. I'm also forty-six-years-old, so whatever I may or may not have been taught in the dim and distant past, there's no excuse for not having rectified any gaps in my Scottish literary education in the intervening period.

Most importantly, there's no excuse for having ignored what turns out to be a great book. Scottish crime writers are renowned the world over – think Ian Rankin, Denise Mina and Val McDermid, to name but three – and McIlvanney is often cited as the godfather of what is called 'tartan noir'. Apparently he hates that title, although is probably more appreciative of McDermid's description of him as 'the Clark Gable of Scottish crime fiction'. Laidlaw is a captivating character, and it's refreshing to read a book where I recognise the setting, even if it does involve a trip down memory lane to recall a Glasgow that doesn't exist any longer.

From McIlvanney's Glasgow of the 1970s, which I know I will return to later, I move to twenty-first century Nova Scotia and *The Bishop's Man* by Linden MacIntyre. This is a novel whose back-cover synopsis definitely caught my eye. It tells the story of a Catholic priest who, over many years, acts as a trouble-shooter for his bishop, heading to parishes where there are reports of scandal involving clergy and helping to cover it up, including claims of child abuse. Given the ongoing scandal of child abuse in the Catholic Church and its attempts to cover it up over many, many years, the subject matter is, sadly, topical.

It's a difficult subject, as a Catholic, to come to terms with. The only phrase that keeps coming into my head is 'There but for the grace of God...' It could have happened in my parish, perhaps even to me, if a paedophile priest had been moved there to get away from a potential scandal elsewhere.

It hasn't undermined my core belief in God, but who couldn't find their faith in the Catholic Church tottering, if not completely collapsing? It is against this backdrop that I read *The Bishop's Man*, a powerful and moving story that gives an 'insider's view' of how the Church deals with its errant priests. I would recommend the book which, though only a work of fiction, contains enough truth within it to ensure I remain unsettled, uncomfortable and angry with my Church.

There is a strange dichotomy with social media. On the one hand, as David Nicholls points out, '... *no-one reaches the end of their life and wishes they'd spent more time on Twitter.*' Indeed, an hour on Twitter can pass by in the blink of an eye, where you have literally done nothing, and literally nothing in the world has happened, except that someone has cooked something tasty on *Masterchef* or there's been a goal in the Barnet versus Plymouth Argyle game. On the other hand, it's an important platform for any writer and provides a gateway to a wider audience. Indeed, you may even be reading these words through a link I've posted on Twitter or Facebook. And I do have Twitter to thank for my next book.

A friend of mine tweets randomly about the comedic genius of P.G. Wodehouse and his *'Jeeves & Wooster'* series of books. I confess that I've never read P.G. Wodehouse. Not that I'm alone in this, and I hadn't really envisaged myself ever doing so. I don't think my life would be any better or worse either way, but the Wodehouse fan is someone whose taste and judgement I respect, and so I ask for a recommendation. I duly purchase *The Code of the Woosters*, and I couldn't have picked a book with a greater contrast to *The Bishop's Man*.

It is entertaining, in a farcical, upper-class twit sort of way, that veers between being funny and infuriating. The biggest drama of the book is about a cow creamer which every character covets. I don't even know what a cow creamer is. *The Code of the Woosters* doesn't convert me to being a Wodehouse fanatic, although I may read more in the future, old chap.

While not necessarily a P.G. Wodehouse fan, I am most definitely a Molly Ringwald devotee. I was a teenager in the 1980s, for goodness sake, so how can I not be? *Pretty in Pink.* *The Breakfast Club.* Need I say more? I discover she's written a novel and so, intrigued at the thought of a celebrity actually writing something rather than taking a suitcase of cash to put their name to something trite – and that can be Cockney rhyming slang if you want – I buy the book.

When It Happens To You is a series of inter-connected stories set in California, and it's deceptively captivating. Molly Ringwald can write. Should I be surprised? I don't know her so I have no idea as to her literary talents, or any other talents beyond an ability to put make-up on with the lipstick wedged in her cleavage, or to dance quite badly to *We Are Not Alone* by Karla DeVito. So I might have watched *The Breakfast Club* more than once. Having finished reading *When It Happens To You*, the book does leave me wanting to know more about the characters and what happens to them, which is a great skill in itself, just giving the reader a glimpse of a life at some random point and then leaving with a lot of loose ends behind. Frustratingly satisfying, I look forward to reading more of her novels in the future. I'm tempted, for about five minutes, to 'tweet' Molly Ringwald and let her know I like the book. I 'follow' her on Twitter. Sad but true. However, I decide against it. There is a fine line between admiration and adulation, and at my age, it's best I don't risk crossing from one to the other. I opt to watch *Pretty in Pink* instead.

I've almost reached the end of January and I'm about to start my ninth book since Boxing Day. That, in itself, is an invigorating thought, and for my next book I decide to tackle my first Sherlock Holmes novel. I have a box-set of all Arthur Conan Doyle's Holmes books, and they have remained in pristine condition on my shelves since I bought them several years ago. The obvious choice is the first book in the series, *A Study In Scarlet*, which sees Holmes and Doctor Watson united for the first time. It's interesting, and easy to read, and clever enough. I believe there are better

Sherlock Holmes books and I may investigate further, but for now it feels like I've ticked another 'should read' novelist off my list. I finish the Conan Doyle book on February 1, and allow myself a moment of self-congratulation. I've read nine books. That is a remarkable total, even if I say so myself, and so I begin February imbued with a new-found literary enthusiasm.

From Starks Park To Seventh Avenue

'I love the solitude of being on a plane and finally getting to read an entire book and being left alone.'

Christina Ricci

It might be worth explaining at this point that I work as a journalist in the multi-media department of Celtic Football Club, writing about the team that I support. It's why, on the second day of February, I find myself in Kirkcaldy, at Starks Park, home of Raith Rovers. It's a cold and chilly Saturday afternoon, and the thought of a fish supper for dinner when I get home later is the only thing enabling me to maintain a cheery disposition in the face of a biting Fife wind.

Our pre-match routine follows a similar pattern – searching out a suitable venue for a fried breakfast and then arrival at the ground two hours before kick-off. While this makes for a long day, the additional time has come in handy on occasion if there are any technical difficulties. I hasten to add that I never have any technical difficulties since I have no idea how anything works, but my colleagues do sometimes encounter a few problems, and the two-hour cushion can be invaluable. As for fried breakfasts, I now like to think of myself as something of a connoisseur. Black pudding is always the key. If it has been freshly cooked, is nice and soft when you cut into it and just about crumbles in your mouth, then you know you're on to a winner. For future reference, in my experience the best eateries are Renfrew Golf Club and Oz's Café in Edinburgh. The fact that the food in both establishments is served on a giant plate may have slightly influenced my decision.

Unfortunately, the early 12.45pm kick-off in Kirkcaldy, and our need to be at the ground two hours beforehand, has a knock-on effect on our routine. So, instead of searching out a suitable venue for a freshly-cooked fry-up, we have to make-do with an ASDA breakfast. It's edible and filling, but the fact that the food's cooked in bulk and left on hot plates means that it's a hit or miss when it's served. Decidedly average is the verdict.

Having devoured nine books since Boxing Day, I'm into double figures at the beginning of February, and the book I take with me to the game is *Ride With The Devil* by Daniel Woodrell. The novel, set during the American Civil War, was originally called *Woe To Live On*, and was made into a film with the new (and better) title. I've actually watched it before reading the book, and it is a fine film which features, among others, a young Toby Maguire and the exquisitely beautiful singer, Jewel. I bought the book on the back of the film, but had never got round to reading it 'til now. Sound familiar? The novel tells the story of a group of Southern militiamen – Bushwhackers – who conduct an increasingly brutal and desperate guerrilla campaign during the war.

With almost two hours to kill until the game kicks off, I sit in the commentary gantry at Starks Park, probably the most sheltered spot in the ground, and begin reading *Ride With The Devil*. That night I finish it. I'm amazed with myself, and tell anyone who'll listen, or pretend to, that I read a whole book in a day. I think I was still at St. Helen's Primary and wearing grey flannel shorts to school every day the last time I managed to achieve that task. I am suitably chuffed. It should come as no surprise to learn that I enjoyed Woodrell's novel. Why else would I have spent so much of Saturday engrossed in it?

It has also reignited the debate over what is better – the book or the film? Actually, there is no debate, since every sane and sensible person knows that the book is always better, even when it's not, just because it's a book. I can't actually think of any occasion where I've preferred the film version of the story to the written one. Some of you may have examples. Some of you may even email those examples to me. I await your correspondence with interest, but remember my 'LOL' rule. *Ride With The Devil* is a very good film, incidentally, and the DVD is now on my mental (as in, my mind, not crazy) list of things to purchase.

Reading a book every day would be an impressive achievement. I also suspect it's an impossible one, even if I was able to devote all my waking hours to this task. My next choice of book confirms this, as well as reminding me that it's not a race I'm taking part in or a competition with anyone else to see who can read the most books in a year. Jane Austen's novel, *Pride and Prejudice,* was first published in 1813 and there has been a healthy amount of publicity surrounding its two-hundredth anniversary. So it's with this in mind that I opt to read it. I've always dismissively considered authors like Austen and the Bronte sisters to be the preserve of female readers, and I never imagined I would ever tackle one of their books. I suspect it's because I have become emboldened by the fact I read nine books in January – NINE – and I finished a whole book in a single day – A DAY – that I feel ready to tackle some nineteenth century 'chick lit'.

That's effectively what *Pride and Prejudice* is. Sorry if there are any Jane Austen fans reading this who might be offended, but that's the impression I get. I'm not saying this as a criticism because I actually enjoy it, and it does continually amaze me that I'm reading something which is two hundred years old. To have stood such a test of time is, in itself, a remarkable achievement, and the style of writing is both of its time and surprisingly easy to read now. The etiquette of nineteenth-century courtship and the attitude towards a woman's place in society is fascinating and this is another book which makes me feel better for having read it.

Having never before considered reading Jane Austen, I have also resisted the appeal of any TV costume dramas based on such classic works of literature. It gives me no 'Colin Firth as Mr D'Arcy' frame of reference, but I believe that to be a good thing. Reading *Pride and Prejudice* also leads to another strange press box conversation with a Scottish football journalist. This time I'm in Inverness and, again, have plenty of time to kill before the game starts. I'm sitting reading *Pride and Prejudice* when one of my journalistic peers walks past me. He halts a few yards away and then heads back along the row, stopping in front of me.

'Lost in Austen,' he says.

I look up. I suppose I am, though it actually might just be that I look tired because it's another early kick-off.

'Have you seen Lost in Austen?' he asks.

I have no idea what he's talking about. He explains that it's a TV series about a twentieth-century obsessive Jane Austen fan who finds herself propelled back to the nineteenth century *Pride and Prejudice* setting. Or at least, I think that's what it's about. My colleague is quite vague about it, not least because he says I have to finish the book before watching the TV series. It's friendly advice rather than an order, and he explains that I'll better appreciate the jokes and references in the show. I thank him for the recommendation, and file it, mentally, under 'TV Series That I Will Never Watch.'

The trials and tribulations of Elizabeth Bennet and her quest for love some two hundred years ago occupy my reading time for more than a single day, but having finally finished it, and concluding for definite that Austen is the 'godmother of chick lit', I opt for a complete contrast, and choose a contemporary thriller – well, it's set in the 1990s – by John Gordon Sinclair. If you're thinking his name is familiar, it might be that you too are a fan of the classic Scottish film, *Gregory's Girl*, in which Mr. Sinclair stars as the eponymous Gregory. If you have seen the film, you'll know that it is simply wonderful. If you haven't seen it, I want to know why not?

Seventy Times Seven is Sinclair's first foray into fiction, and I am intrigued to find out how he's got on. The novel is set between Ireland and America, and involves Irish republicans, American gangsters and Mexican drug lords. It's a page-turner, which I sometimes worry is a polite way of saying that it's an average, easy-to-read book that encourages you to turn the page quickly so that the experience can be over sooner rather than later. The book is more than that, and the bulk of *Seventy Times Seven* is very much a captivating thriller. The ending is a bit contrived and convoluted and is not totally satisfactory, however, and does leave me with the impression that 'Gregory' had 'Hollywood blockbuster' in mind when he wrote it. That, in itself, is not a criticism because if the book does become a film, I will doff my cap to Mr. Sinclair for achieving something I haven't.

I'm almost three weeks into February and I've only read three books. It means I have no chance of replicating my impressive January tally, but since 'quality not quantity' is my new mantra, I don't get too disheartened. I also have a good distraction in the shape of an impending trip to New York. It's three years since my first trip to the Big Apple, and having had the most wonderful time back in 2010, my excitement at the return visit rises the closer it gets to our departure date. I've also decided to take my Kindle rather than packing any books into the suitcase.

I enjoyed reading books on the Kindle the previous summer, and the fact that I can hold over one hundred books in the palm of my hand remains a twenty-first century phenomenon I still occasionally find difficult to comprehend, just as I adore my iPod, but can't quite get my head round the fact I have fifteen thousand, eight hundred and twenty-seven songs in my pocket. However, I love books. I really do. I love the feel of them, how they look. Before I lost my sense of smell, I loved their odour too. I will always come down on the side of the physical book rather than the e-book and so, for me, the Kindle is a handy holiday accoutrement, but it is one that I do like. It also gives my luggage allowance a healthy boost.

Our plane takes off from Glasgow Airport at nine o'clock on the morning of Thursday, February 21, on a direct flight to Newark Airport. At thirty-thousand feet, I start reading *The Hangman's Daughter* by Oliver Potzsch. The story is set in seventeenth century Germany, and is a dark tale involving an executioner and torturer in Bavaria, Jakob Kuisl, who has to investigate a series of child murders in his town that are being blamed on witchcraft and the influence of the devil. Kuisl does this with the help of his feisty daughter, hence the title of the book, and the son of the local doctor, who also happens to be in love with the hangman's daughter. It's a thrillingly-written story, beautifully laced with fine historical details, and I discover later that the author is, in fact, descended from a line of executioners, including Jakob Kuisl, though the story in *The Hangman's Daughter* is fictional. It is the first in a trilogy of books featuring the same characters, and with the other two also downloaded on to the Kindle, I know I will return to seventeenth century Bavaria.

The book also provides a welcome distraction during the six hours, forty-five minutes I'm in the air since, if I think about it, I'll probably slip into a catatonic state at the realisation of how high up I am. Flying is not natural, unless you're a bird. It's a necessary evil, otherwise I'll never get to see the world, or parts of it, but my favourite moment is always when the wheels hit the runway on landing and I know that I've lived to fly another day.

The fact that Oliver Potzsch's novel is so riveting also helps take my mind off the guy sitting next to me who keeps ordering double gins every time a stewardess passes by. His credit card has been permanently stuck at the side of the small TV screen on the back of the seat in front, and I'm tempted at various times to either try and snap it 'accidentally' when I get out of my seat to go to the toilet, or when the guy answers the call of nature I want to scribble the card details down, including the three-digit security code on the back of the card so that I will later be able to buy lots of useless but expensive stuff on the Internet using his account. In the end, I do neither, since I am not malicious or malevolent,

Even with the Kindle, I still eventually need to put headphones on to drown out the increasingly drunken mutterings of my neighbour. I watch a film, *Ruby Sparks*, about a young writer who is struggling to write a new novel following the success of his first book. He has a dream about a girl, Ruby Sparks, and starts writing about her and how he's falling in love with her. Mysteriously, she comes to life and appears in his apartment. I'll not spoil the film for you, not least because I can't be bothered explaining all the intricacies of the plot, but it's an enjoyable and quirky film which makes for a refreshing addition to the romantic comedy genre of which I am an aficionado.

New York is wonderful. If you've ever visited the city you'll know what I mean, and if you don't like it, then you're a strange person who is unlikely to find much joy in life. It has a familiarity about it, even though much of it is completely new. The city forms such an integral part of many of our cultural references, from *Breakfast At Tiffany's* and *An Affair To Remember* to the ubiquitous *Friends* TV series that, while it's not quite like coming home, it doesn't take long to find your bearings. The lay-out of the city, with its logical grid pattern of streets and avenues, also helps, and having been in New York before, we instantly know our way about.

We're staying at the Wellington Hotel on Seventh Avenue at 55th Street, and our room on the twenty-sixth floor offers a breathtaking view down Seventh Avenue, no matter what time of the day or night we look out the window. I'm not just saying that to sound like a contributor to TripAdvisor. It truly is stunning, and it provides a memorable vista to enjoy while tackling my next book.

Having finished *The Hangman's Daughter* within a couple of days, I turn to Richard Ford's latest novel, *Canada*. Richard Ford is one of my favourite writers and The *Sportswriter* is a novel that I have read on several occasions. It's the first part of the Frank Bascombe trilogy, which also includes *Independence Day* and *The Lay of the Land*, and I can't recommend the books highly enough. Ford writes beautifully and effortlessly. I realised, from the moment I read the first few lines of *The Sportswriter*, that I would never be able to write anything that would come anywhere near his standard.

'My name is Frank Bascombe. I am a sportswriter. For the past

*fourteen years I have lived here at 19 Hoving Road, Haddam, New
Jersey, in a large Tudor house bought when a book of short stories I
wrote sold to a movie producer for a lot of money, and seemed to set my
wife and me and our three children – two of whom were not even born yet
– up for a good life.*

*Just exactly what that good life was – the one I expected – I cannot
tell you now exactly, though I wouldn't say that it has not come to pass,
only that much has come in between. I am no longer married to X, for
instance. The child we had when everything was starting has died, though
there are two others, as I mentioned, who are alive and wonderful
children.'*

To paraphrase a line from the film, *Jerry Maguire*, you had
me at *'My name'*. Occasionally, over the years, I have found
the thought of never being that good a disheartening one, but
most of the time I accept my own talent, and its limitations,
and just enjoy the brilliance of Richard Ford. *Canada* does not
disappoint. The book begins: *'First, I'll tell about the robbery our
parents committed. Then the murders, which happened later.'* Now
that's a first sentence to envy. I'm already hooked, and the
story of Dell Parsons' family woes and how he ended up in
the eponymous Canada of the book is a stunningly-told one. I
recommend it to you all, in much the same way that I would
recommend any Richard Ford book.

I enjoy the novel on its own merits, but I have to confess
that the reading experience is enhanced by my location. Every
day I wake up about seven o'clock, with the early morning
New York sunshine desperately trying to burst through the
thin curtain we've pulled across the window. I can see and
hear the city awake already – yes, I know I'm in the city that
never sleeps – and after soaking up our stunning view once
again, I lie in bed reading *Canada* for an hour. I have a cover
for my Kindle which includes a small reading light, a welcome
accessory that ensures I don't disturb Karen.

As I mentioned before, I consider myself to be an expert
on Scottish fried breakfasts, and I have the waistline to prove
it, and while that culinary delight will always remain close to

my heart, probably hardening my arteries with every serving, I have also fallen in love with New York breakfasts. Starting the day with a plate of corned beef hash and fried potatoes and as many refills of black coffee as my bladder can cope with is the best way to tackle the hours of sightseeing ahead, and the diner nearest our hotel is our first port of call every morning. I have also fallen in love with the New York subway, and the seven-day, twenty-eight dollar Metro card we each buy for unlimited travel around the city is the best purchase of the trip. I rave about it so much that, on our last day, Karen buys me a fridge magnet in the shape of a Metro ticket. It's a lovely gesture, but it's on the strength of such tiny moments that strange, unusual and disturbing collections are often born.

While we've planned to do the usual checklist of tourist activities such as the Empire State Building, Times Square, Ground Zero Memorial and Central Park – the Statue of Liberty remains closed due to the damage caused by Hurricane Sandy back in October 2012 – I also want to visit a book shop. Yes, I have travelled three thousand, two hundred and twenty-one miles just so that I can go into a book shop and wander round. This isn't any old book shop, however. On the recommendation of a friend of mine, Hugh MacDonald of *The Herald* newspaper, I seek out The Strand Book Store at the corner of 12th Street and Broadway.

'You have to visit The Strand,' Hugh tells me before my trip. 'It's an incredible place. It has eighteen miles of books.'

The scale of that is beyond my comprehension, and I envisage a book shop the size of a football pitch. My God, that would be bibliophile heaven. It sounds like hell to Karen. Our arrangement, therefore, is that on the Saturday morning, while she goes to check out the sale at Macy's Department Store, I head for The Strand. That's all well and good but, on coming out of a Metro station at 12th Street, I go west when I should have gone east, and so, instead of coming upon the store within a couple of minutes, I walk for nearly fifteen minutes before I realise what I've done. I'm tired, wet, I'm not singing in the rain and I'm slightly disheartened. However, out of adversity comes triumph, and I achieve another ambition of travelling in a yellow New York cab when I flag one down and get him to take me to The Strand.

The Athenian statesman, Aristides, who was nicknamed 'The Just', made an astute comment regarding book shops, which is not really surprising given that he was also described as 'the best and most honourable man in Athens'. Writing at some point between 530BC and 468BC, Aristides said:

'One of the tests of a good city is the quality of its bookstores.'

These are wise words, and it does make me think about Glasgow. There is a real paucity of good book shops, and while a few lurk in the suburban shadows, the city does not have any flagship or famous independent stores that draw readers from far and wide. It's something that I wish my city would try to rectify.

While Aristide's words remain etched in my mind – admittedly, I had to 'Google' the quote – it is Reece Witherspoon's observation which has more resonance as I stand inside The Strand and try to get my bearings. Yes, I'm talking about *that* Reece Witherspoon, star of films such as *Cruel Intentions, Election, Sweet Home Alabama, Walk The Line* and, of course, the wonderful *Legally Blonde* and its sequel, *Legally Blonde 2: Red, White & Blonde*. She said:

'I get crazy in a bookstore. It makes my heart beat hard because I want to buy everything.'

I know what she means, although I have to qualify that by saying, if I saw Reece Witherspoon in a bookstore, I would go crazy and my heart would beat hard. Sadly, she is not in The Strand when I visit, and so I have to make do with browsing through the books.

From the outside the shop looks unremarkable, and even when I step inside, I'm not immediately blown away by the scale of it. It's only as I venture further into its bowels that I realise the shelves do indeed stretch for miles, and contain thousands upon thousands of new and used books all sitting patiently waiting for a new owner. Stacked from floor to ceiling it feels at first like all the books ever published have been crammed into the store which occupies 55,000 square feet of space. I've done my research, in case you're wondering. I haven't turned up at the shop armed with a very large tape measure.

The Strand is full of people scanning the shelves, checking out staff recommendations on the tables which clutter the floor space, or queuing up at the back of the store to sell their unwanted books, waiting while a member of staff expertly examines each book and then, almost dismissively, gives a verdict, and a price.

The books vastly outnumber the customers so at no time do I feel it is too busy or claustrophobic. Is this how New Zealanders feel when surrounded by so many sheep? There are people like me, middle-aged men who have managed to avoid Saturday morning shopping with their partner, The Strand offering a brief but welcome respite from the chores of domesticity. There are older people, grey-haired men and women carrying stacks of books. They could almost be mistaken for members of staff. They are serious readers, their life spent devouring words. There are younger customers too. A group of girls, loud and vivacious as only young women can be. They're probably students. Occasional glances of disdain are thrown in their direction by others who feel the tranquillity of their browsing has been unnecessarily disturbed, but I think their presence is a good sign. Like the cry of a baby in church during Mass, it's a sound and sign that the art of reading and a love of books are still flourishing amongst the next generation.

There are native New Yorkers in The Strand, their visit probably part of a weekly post-breakfast ritual, while there is a veritable cornucopia of accents floating up towards the top of the book-shelves. They could all be New Yorkers too, since the city is an enviable and exciting cocktail of cultures. I don't think my pasty-faced complexion has marked me down as Scottish. I am just another book lover and potential book buyer. My presence is neither remarked upon nor is remarkable.

I wish, too, that the sense of smell which mysteriously disappeared without me ever noticing would return now and the aroma of the books, new and old mixing together, the blend cogitating over time, would rush up my nose and infuse me with dizzying memories of all the books which have passed through my hands. It doesn't happen, of course, although my sense of touch remains intact and I pick out a few paperbacks just to caress the covers. American-published paperbacks have a different feel to them, like the cover has been coated with a material that gives it a sense of superiority over its trans-Atlantic cousins.

The hour I have in the shop before meeting up with Karen isn't nearly long enough. It would have been longer, of course, if I hadn't wasted part of the time heading in the wrong direction, but I could have spent a whole day here, looking through the shelves for an hour and then popping out for a coffee at a nearby diner before returning to resume my browsing. I also find that being on my feet for so long is beginning to hurt my back – I'm forty-six, for goodness sake, so show some sympathy – and there's nowhere inside the store to rest my weary body.

In the end I only buy three books. Part of that is because I hadn't planned on packing my suitcase for the trip home with books and also because it's actually harder to select what to buy from such a wide choice. My mind has temporarily erased all the books and authors I want to read and so I wander blindly along each row, studying the shelves in the hope that something will jump out at me. I'm like a small child on Christmas Day, overwhelmed by the never-ending deluge of presents to the point where I'll either burst into tears or end up playing with an empty cardboard box.

I choose *The Last Storyteller* by Frank Delaney. I've read a previous book of his, *Ireland – A Novel*, which is a stunning story, so I have high hopes for this one. The other two novels are both by Gil Scott-Heron – *The Vulture* and *The Nigger Factory*. He was an American soul and jazz poet, musician and author, who died in 2011. His dad, Gil Heron, also happens to be an ex-Celtic footballer, who was briefly at the club between 1951 and '52 and has the distinction of being Celtic's first black player. It might be a flimsy connection but it's enough to confirm the purchase. There are three copies of *The Vulture* on the shelves, two at the full price of twelve dollars and one at six dollars. There seems to be no discernible difference in the quality, so I feel like I'm getting a bargain as I take the cheaper-priced copy. *The Vulture* suddenly jumps to the top of my list of books to read once I've finished *Canada*, which continues to be my reading companion even when I return home to Glasgow, the resolution also having taken root in my mind that when we next return to New York, I'm going to set a day aside for a proper expedition to The Strand.

Seeing Is Believing

'Beware of the person of one book.'
Saint Thomas Aquinas

The second day of March proves to be an enjoyable one for a number of reasons. Celtic have a game in Paisley, which means a pre-match trip to Renfrew Golf Club for breakfast. None of us are members of the club or, indeed, golfers. In fact, I'm the only one in the multi-media team who doesn't view the sport as 'a good walk spoiled,' to quote Mark Twain. Our connection to this particular golf club is due to family ties – my brother-in-law runs it – and so we're able to experience one of the finest cooked breakfasts that you'll find in the land. Our appetites suitably sated, we're able to enjoy the rest of the day, which includes a Celtic victory.

For me, it also means finishing *Canada*. I already know what I'm going to read next so I've got Gil Scott-Heron's *The Vulture* on my bedside cabinet that night. The Kindle would, in normal circumstances, get an opportunity to metaphorically recharge its batteries before the summer holidays, when I would have to actually recharge the batteries ahead of our trip, but Karen is borrowing it to read a book. And not just any book. It's one that I wrote. It's the second draft of a new novel that I've been working on, tentatively entitled *As Well As Can Be Expected*, and I'm looking for a fresh opinion on it since, by now, I believe it to be a masterpiece of literary perfection.

Have I mentioned already that I've written a trilogy of novels? They're set between Scotland, Ireland and the United States, and take place in the years spanning 1891 to 1922. I wanted to try something completely different and so this new, yet-to-be published book has a contemporary setting. It's partly Karen's fault for me writing it. I gave her a list of eight ideas, with a brief description of each. *As Well As Can Be Expected* was the one she liked the most. I've already read a draft of it on my Kindle. It's great being able to convert the Word document and transfer it on to the Kindle so that I can go through the entire novel and get the experience of reading it as a book, if that makes sense. I'm still 'old school' when it comes to actually editing it, so I'll print out the manuscript and have my red pen at the ready when I pour over each page in the hunt for every mistake I've made. I know that they're lurking there, trying to hide from me. I'm afraid there's only one infallible Catholic in the world, and it's not me, although events in the Church during March, with the retirement of Pope Benedict and election of his successor, Pope Francis, means that there are now two infallible Catholics in the world, neither of whom are me.

While Karen starts reading my book, I delve into *The Vulture*. In the novel, a teenage drug dealer has been killed, and in four separate sections of the narrative, four characters tell their story and their connection to the victim, leading, in the end, to the reader finding out who the killer is. I have to remind myself throughout the novel that all the protagonists are teenagers, some of them still at school, but their immersion in a life of sex, drugs, alcohol and violence makes them seem older.

Reading *The Vulture*, I find myself transported back to 1970s New York, the descriptions of which are both familiar and alien to me, mostly the latter since I've only visited the city twice and both of these occasions have been in the past three years. The city has changed a lot in the past forty-three years. The book reminds me of comments I heard from the writer and social commentator, Fran Lebowitz, who is a New Yorker. Speaking in a Martin Scorsese-directed documentary about her life, *Public Speaking*, Lebowitz said of her city today:

'New York was not better because there was more crime. It was better because it was cheaper and I mean relatively cheaper. When a place is too expensive, only people with lots of money can live there.

That's the problem. You can like people with lots of money for certain reasons, you can hate them for certain reasons but you cannot say an entire city of people with lots of money is fascinating. It is not. All these things, in my opinion, seemed to occur when they decided to get the city out of bankruptcy by making it into a tourist attraction, which everyone seems to think was the smartest thing ever done. In other words, in the 1970s when the city was going bankrupt, three guys got together and said 'What can we do? The city is going bankrupt. Well, no-one here can think of anything, so we'll just have to bring a lot of people here to come and look at it.'

It was an incredibly horrible idea, and even at the time I thought, 'This is New York City - if you don't want to come here, good. Don't come here.' It was a very bad thing because it made it seem like New York had no resources, and by that I mean human resources. It wasn't like New York was a boring place. You cannot lure these hordes of hillbillies into the centre of a city and not have it affect the city. It's not possible.

What would we do with Times Square if there were no tourists? I mean, it's a place we built for them. It used to just be a neighbourhood. I live near Times Square, and here's what we could use in this neighbourhood – a butcher, a shoe-repairer, a stationary store, a book store. You could fill it with things New Yorkers need. Here's what it's like in Times Square in the last few years. If you're a New Yorker and you run into another New Yorker in Times Square, it's like running into someone in a gay bar in the seventies. You instantly start making excuses for why you're there.'

The comments are provocative, deliberately so, and offer an interesting perspective on the city and its transformation to attract people like me into visiting. New York is my second-favourite place to visit after Rome, which I think is wonderful. Well, actually, my favourite city in the world in Glasgow, which I love, since it is home. Lebowitz's observations, along with reading *The Vulture*, make me reflect on Glasgow's transformation since the 1970s – the setting of McIlvanney's *Laidlaw* which I'd read back in January, and which forms my earliest memories of the city. There has been an incredible transformation, certainly over the past thirty years, in terms of lay-out, retail development and social movement in Glasgow though, unlike New York, I believe it has been motivated, first and foremost, by a desire to make the city a better place for Glaswegians. Any boost to tourist numbers has just been a welcome bonus.

You may have guessed by now that I like to vary the books I'm reading, whether that's in terms of genre, style or setting. So having finished Gil Scott-Heron's crime novel set on New York's mean streets, I turn to *Billionaire Boy* by David Walliams. The comedian, best known for the *Little Britain* TV series with Matt Lucas, has written a number of children's books, all of which have been critically and commercially acclaimed. In part because I have the kernel of an idea in my mind to write a kids' book, I decide to read Walliams' book, for 'research' purposes, you understand.

It's laugh-out-loud funny, with one of the best punchlines at the end of a book you're ever likely to read. I absolutely love this book. It's funny and clever, with a clear moral in the story, as all good kids' books should have, but there are also enough elements within it to amuse and entertain any parents reading it to their children. The book is illustrated by Quentin Blake, who famously was the illustrator for the legendary Roald Dahl's kids' books, and it's clear there is a Dahl influence in Walliams' story. That's no bad thing, since Roald Dahl was a genius. *Charlie and the Chocolate Factory* is one of my favourite books from childhood, and remains so even now, having read it in adulthood and loved it still.

Last year, I discovered a website that sold genuine Wonka Bars, which was like the answer to all my childhood dreams. If only there was a website which sold former *Blue Peter* presenter Sarah Greene, circa 1983 ... That would be the answer to all my teenage wet dreams. Any mention of *Charlie and the Chocolate Factory* can also provoke a great pub/office/family debate. Which is the better film adaptation of the book – the 1971 Gene Wilder version, or the more recent 2005 Johnny Depp film? I'll leave that one with you.

Billionaire Boy is another book which only takes me a day to read, although I don't look on this with the same sense of achievement as I did when I demolished *Ride With The Devil,* but Walliams' book is already near the top of the charts for my favourite books that I've read so far in 2013 and I have a feeling it will stay there throughout the course of the year.

Next up for me is *A Fan's Notes* by Frederick Exley. It's one of those books where there appears to be a blurred line between fact and fiction. Is it just a novel or the author's memoir? It tells the story of a sports fan who is obsessed with the New York Giants American football team. At the start of the book the main character is estranged from his wife and children and he's drinking heavily. He is also instantly dislikeable, and within a short space of time, I despise him so much that I can't read any more. I'm not enjoying the book, I don't care about the character and what happens to him, and I can see this experience stretching out for weeks and weeks, with the risk that my resurgent enthusiasm for reading will drain away. So I decide to quit while I'm ahead.

I know there are two camps of readers – those who will always finish a book, regardless of the level of enjoyment and those who, like me, will give up. My reasoning is that life is too short and there are too many good books, never mind great books still to read, to waste time on something that I'm not enjoying.

I remember buying *The Satanic Verses* back in 1989. It wasn't long after the fatwa was issued against Salman Rushdie, and I bought the book to show my solidarity with Rushdie, seeing the purchase as a declaration of my support for the fundamental right to free speech. I even tried reading it a couple of times, but on both occasions I gave up fairly early into the book. The last time I tried reading it was in November 1993. I got to page ninety-one. I know this because the bookmark, an old bus pass, still rests in that page. As for the date, a newspaper cutting I've placed inside the front of the book reveals that to me. It was a column written by Benedict Brogan on November 4, 1993. Brogan now writes for the *Daily Telegraph*, but at the time he worked for the *Glasgow Herald*. His column seemed to be written specifically for me. I cut it out, put it into *The Satanic Verses*, and slipped the book back on to my shelves, never to be opened again until now, as I re-read Brogan's words:

'Take a deep breath. Now say with me: 'I have never finished a Salman Rushdie novel.' Go on. There's no shame in it. You'll feel much better, I promise. Say it out loud, then do something about that copy of The Satanic Verses on the bedside table. You know, the one you bought years ago when supporting Salman was fashionable? 'I have never finished a Salman Rushdie novel.' I admitted it publicly for the first time last Saturday, all thanks to my friend Paddy. He was talking about Roddy Doyle and the Booker Prize when he mentioned it, in an aside as casual as turning a page; he has never made it to the end of Shame or Midnight's Children, and was not embarrassed to admit it.

We paused in a moment of stunned, mutual recognition. Then it all came tumbling out. How I had bought Shame years ago, started it, read through the first 100 pages or so and then somehow came adrift. How the same thing happened with Midnight's Children. How both still sit on the shelves I reserve for 'books to read one day'. How by the time Satanic Verses appeared I was too embarrassed to try again. It was pure, delightful therapy. My burden of guilt, of dinner party conversations peppered with fraudulent declarations of admiration for Rushdie's genius, of recommendations dishonestly given, lifted like a veil.

Since Saturday I have been contemplating all those books I have never read, and all the ones I started with the best of intentions, never to reach the final page. What were once secrets, hidden away safely in my subconscious, far from the prying eyes of my well-read friends, can now be revealed.'

Having put Exley's book away for now or, more likely, for ever, I turn to Jane Harris' novel, *Gillespie and I*. Having really enjoyed her debut novel, *The Observations*, I have high hopes for this one. I'm not disappointed. Set mainly in Glasgow in the late nineteenth-century, though occasionally jumping forward to 1933, it's a strange and chilling tale that is part murder mystery but also, for me, an intriguing reflection on the uniquely Scottish 'Not Proven' verdict that Sir Walter Scott described as 'that bastard verdict.' For those of you not familiar with the Scottish legal system, it basically means that a jury in Scotland has three options available to choose from – 'Guilty', 'Not Guilty' and 'Not Proven'. I could go into the historical roots of this, or offer an explanation of what each one means in legal terms, but I have neither the time, inclination nor the expertise. Put simply, for Scottish people, 'Not Proven' means that the person is guilty but the prosecution hasn't been able to prove this 'beyond reasonable doubt'. *Gillespie and I* is a thought-provoking novel, and confirms Jane Harris as a fine writer.

The news that Roddy Doyle, another of my favourite authors, has been nominated for the Carnegie Medal, a prestigious award for children's fiction, provokes my interest. The book nominated is *A Greyhound of a Girl*, and I immediately buy it. I think Roddy Doyle is one of literature's most talented storytellers. From the Barrytown trilogy (*The Commitments, The Snapper, The Van*) through to *A Star Called Henry* and *The Deportees,* along with many publications in between, he has been a prolific writer of many wonderful books. My own particular favourite is the 1993 Booker Prize-winning novel, *Paddy Clarke Ha Ha Ha.* I know he's written a few kids' books before, but *A Greyhound of a Girl* appears to be aimed at the young adult market.

It is impossible to fully describe just how beautiful this story is. There are four main female characters in the book – a daughter, mother, grandmother and a ghost – which is an exquisite tale and a celebration of Irish family and femininity, though I'm sure it would translate to any country or culture. I'm in a quandary when I finish it. On the one hand, I want to give it to everyone I know since it's such a wonderful book, but at the same time I'm loathe to let my copy out of my sight. At the moment, it remains in my possession, but I know I should share it. I will. Probably.

It is at this time of the month, March 21 to be exact, that

the death of renowned Nigerian writer Chinua Achebe is announced. I read his most famous novel, *Things Fall Apart*, a few years ago, but hearing of his passing makes me want to read it again. One of the first African novels to be widely translated into English, it is an extraordinary book and tells the story of Okonkwo, a local wrestling champion in his village. The novel examines the culture clash between traditional Nigerian values and those of the Christian missionaries and colonialists who arrive in the country in the nineteenth century.

A couple of days after I start reading it, I'm in ASDA buying a heat spray for Karen who has pulled a muscle in her shoulder. For reasons known only to the ASDA store bosses, they have placed reading glasses right beside the heat sprays, and something makes me take a pair of glasses from the shelf – actually, it's a packet of two for two pounds – and buy them. I already own a pair of glasses, which cost considerably more than two pounds. I no longer use them. I'm not actually sure where they are. I got them about five years ago after I kept getting headaches at work while using the computer. They seemed to work, for a while at least, although I found that actually getting up from my work station a few times a day was just as helpful.

Effectively, the reading glasses just magnify the type on the page, which immediately helps me in finishing *Things Fall Apart*. It also gives me an idea for my next book choice. I have a copy of *Confederates* by Thomas Keneally, which I've wanted to read for years, but the type is too small and squashed together, and I'd all but given up hope of ever reading it. Now, wearing my reading glasses – at 1.5+ strength – I feel ready to tackle it. The only problem I have is in locating it.

I have thousands of books, as I might have mentioned once or twice, but they are in no order, so any time I want to find a book I have to search every shelf, often turning them all upside down in order to locate what I'm looking for. It's not been unknown for my search to be a fruitless one even though I know the book is there, somewhere. So one Sunday afternoon I decide to alphabetise my collection. I want to put them in a general order – a shelf for each letter is my starting point. Proper alphabetisation can wait for another day. At one point during the proceedings, with every book dumped on the dining room floor so that it's like an obstacle course when I try to move about, I take a break, already fed up with my task and wondering whatever possessed me to start it.

'Do you think your mum will be annoyed if I just leave all the books lying on the floor?' I ask my eighteen-year-old son, Andrew.

'Probably,' he replies, 'although I don't know why. We hardly ever use the dining room.'

Oh son, if only life was that simple … Eventually, after many hours of blood, sweat and tears, I have my books in some sort of order so that, for example, when Rebecca asks about James Elroy's novel, *The Black Dahlia*, I locate it within seconds. She is almost impressed. Another bonus of my alphabetising activity is that I find *Confederates* and tackle it after finishing Chinua Achebe's novel.

Thomas Keneally's book tells the story of a group of soldiers fighting for Stonewall Jackson's Confederate army during the American Civil War. It's my second novel about this period of history, following on from *Ride With The Devil*, and *Confederates* is a fine book which describes in great detail the brutality of war. I can understand why it was shortlisted for the Booker Prize back in 1979, but what makes the reading experience all the most enjoyable is that it's an unexpected one. Like a blind man whose sight is miraculously restored, the reading glasses allow me to enjoy a book I thought I would never be able to tackle. I apologise for the hyperbole, and also for any offence that blind people might take for this comment.

Keneally is, of course, a brilliant writer, as anyone who has read *Schindler's Ark* can testify; the title was changed to *Schindler's List* for the film. Keneally's American Civil War book takes me into early April. Indeed, on the last day of

March, I make a return journey to Paisley on work duty, which also involves another visit to Renfrew Golf Club and their peerless breakfast. I don't take *Confederates* with me. The previous night, we have a party in the house to celebrate Rebecca's twenty-first birthday. I get to bed at seven o'clock in the morning and I'm back up again at half past eight. I am a very fragile passenger as the car heads to the golf club. The fry-up certainly helps in my recovery, but even with two hours to kill, I know it would be a mistake to try and encourage my brain to read anything, even with the aid of reading glasses.

The following Tuesday there is terrible news, not just for Scottish literature, but for the world of letters as a whole. Iain Banks, who writes novels under his own name and science-fiction books as Iain M. Banks, announces via his website that 'I am officially Very Poorly.' The statement goes on to explain that he has cancer and is terminally ill, with just a few months to live. He is only fifty-nine. A prolific and popular writer in both genres – think *The Wasp Factory* and *The Crow Road* as Iain Banks, or *Use of Weapons* and *The Player of Games* as Iain M. Banks – the news shocks me, and I don't even know him, except through his work. It is one of those 'Carpe Diem' moments, and I resolve to redouble my own writing efforts. Karen has finished reading the draft of my next novel, and gives it the thumbs-up, although when I read it again, it seems to fit the title perfectly – As Well As Can Be Expected. It's back to the drawing, or writing, board for me.

A Kick Up The Eighties

'I suspect any serious reader has a first great book,
just the way anybody has a first kiss.'
Michael Cunningham

I start reading *Espedair Street* on April 6. It is one of several Iain Banks novels that I've owned for a number of years but have never got round to reading. In fact, I have only ever read *The Wasp Factory*, which unsettled me so much I suspect it made me wary of tackling any more of his books and, more recently, *The Crow Road*, which I did after watching the brilliant BBC adaptation of the novel. Banks apparently once described it as being 'annoyingly better than the book.' I can't agree because, for reasons previously mentioned, the book is always better than the film (or TV adaptation), even when it isn't, but in this case, Banks might well be right. I should add that I've also read a couple of his science-fiction books and enjoyed them, which was a pleasant surprise given that it's a genre which is alien to me.

I'm sad while reading the novel, even though it's not really a sad book. *Espedair Street* tells the story of a reclusive rock star who is more or less hiding out in a converted church in Glasgow with more money than he could ever dream of. The story of how he and his band, Frozen Gold, became successful and why he is in his current situation is told in the course of the novel. My sadness comes, of course, from knowing that the author is dying.

On April 8, two days after I start reading *Espedair Street*, I receive a text at 12.54pm from Rebecca. It reads 'Thatcher has died!' At the age of eighty-seven, the former Prime Minister has shuffled off this mortal coil. There are the usual sycophantic tributes from friends and former colleagues, tempered to some degree by scathing criticism from her political enemies and, dare I say it, victims. There is wall-to-wall news coverage, even when every angle of the story has been exhausted, which only serves to highlight the tediousness of twenty-four-hour rolling news channels. There is even a party in Glasgow's George Square. A crowd of around three hundred people gather in the city centre the same night Thatcher dies to 'celebrate' the passing of Britain's first female prime minister, the longest-serving prime minister of the twentieth-century, and one of the most divisive leaders in British political history.

Like many millions of people, I don't believe her 'achievements' should be celebrated nor should we all have to mourn her death, but the scenes of jubilation leave me feeling uncomfortable. I don't believe the death of anyone should be celebrated with a party. If nothing else, everyone who despises everything that Thatcherism stood for should be better than that. We are better than that.

I try to avoid most of the news coverage, although the bulletins I do catch contain some great footage from the 1980s, which takes me back to that era. I was almost thirteen when Thatcher came to power in 1979 and was twenty-four when she was booted out of Downing Street by her own party in 1990. That period constitutes the formative years of my political awareness. I even joined the Labour Party after their 1987 General Election defeat, so disgusted was I that Thatcher was still in power. Thankfully I soon saw sense with that fleeting political allegiance. Thatcher's death makes me think of what her 'reign' helped to produce in cultural terms. I'm finding it hard to think of any good novels from that period. There's plenty of good music, along with a whole raft of powerful films and television programmes; *Boys From The Blackstuff* remains one of British TV's finest hours. Where is literature's contribution to that period?

I turn to Twitter for some help, using a twenty-first century innovation to help me remember a time when there were only three television channels in Britain, no-one knew what a mobile phone was and 'LOL' still meant 'Lots of

Love.' There are a couple of suggestions for *GB84* by David Peace. I've read his brilliant football novel, *The Damned United*, about Brian Clough and his short-lived reign as Leeds United manager in the 1970s, and so I order *GB84*. Another 'tweet' mentions *Boys From The Blackstuff.* I don't have the heart to reply and point out it's not a novel. Someone else suggests *Jurassic Park* by Michael Crichton, saying that the book 'pretty much covers it. Bunch of ancient reptiles let loose on a bunch of innocent men, woman and children. The results ARE not good.'

Espedair Street takes an unexpected turn towards the end of the book, becoming a love story with a schmaltzy Hollywood-style finale which takes me by surprise. Several of Banks' books have been adapted for the big or small screen, so I wonder if he had that in mind when he wrote the conclusion.

Staying true to my aim of trying to vary my reading matter, I throw myself head-first into some contemporary chick-lit. I pick up *Old School Ties* by Kate Harrison as part of a 'Three books for five pounds' offer at Tesco. The cover is classic 'chick-lit' – pastel pink and sky blue – and while I'm one hundred per cent comfortable reading the book, I have to confess that I'm not confident enough to read it in public. I realise this when I take a bus journey into Glasgow to meet a friend and 'bottle' out of taking *Old School Ties* with me just in case I'm spotted. I'm not proud of myself, and I have no excuses for my cowardice.

I like the book. It tells the story of a woman who was the most popular girl at school in the early 1980s. Now unhappily married with two children, she is given the opportunity by a television company to be the central character in a school reunion programme. Those schooldays were the same era as my own, which adds to my enjoyment of the book, while the subject of school reunions is one that I'm sure fascinates many people. It definitely intrigues me.

Stevie Maule and I first became friends in 1981 when we were both fourth-year pupils at Turnbull High School in

Bishopbriggs. Over the years we've wondered what happened to the people we were at school with. If I'm being honest, we really just wonder what happened to the girls and what they look like now; have the years been kind to the ones we considered back then to be the prettiest? I always find this discussion amusing, particularly when I look at myself in the mirror. I'm an overweight, bald, grey-haired, middle-aged man. It's hard to imagine thirty years not having an impact on even the best-looking people from school, of whom I was not one, and I've no doubt all of the girls will have aged much, much better than me.

It doesn't take long to finish *Old School Ties*. Having opted rather bashfully not to tell Molly Ringwald via Twitter that I had enjoyed her novel, I decide, perhaps in part to assuage my guilt at not wanting to be seen reading the book in public, to contact Kate Harrison via email.

Kate,

I just wanted to email and say how much I enjoyed reading 'Old School Ties'. The whole idea of school reunions is one that I find fascinating, intriguing and appalling in equal measures, and I think the book captured it brilliantly. It also made me remember my own school days back in the early 1980s. I'm still friends with someone from school and we occasionally have one of those 'I wonder what happened to...' conversations.

I'm not sure how the book is or should be categorised, or how you see it, although I'm presuming the cover design hints at it being aimed at a 'chick lit' market. Apologies if that's wide of the mark. However, I believe that books shouldn't be classed on gender lines, and a good book is just a good book. 'Old School Ties' just reinforces that belief and I look forward to reading more of your books.

Best wishes.

Paul Cuddihy

PS: I've also been doing the 5:2 Diet for a few months now and I think it's wonderful!

The 5:2 Diet, for anyone who hasn't heard of it, basically

involves not eating for two days out of seven. There are variations – some people will eat one 500-calorie meal in those twenty-four hours, but I prefer not to eat anything. So, for example, after I've eaten my dinner on a Sunday night at six o'clock, I won't eat again until six o'clock on Monday night. During those twenty-four hours I will drink water and black coffee. It's not as difficult or extreme as it might seem, and the benefits are many. Weight loss is the obvious one, which is great when you're still eating a fried breakfast every weekend, while there is also ongoing research into the rejuvenative effects of the 5:2 diet, as it allows your body time to rest and repair itself. There is evidence that it can lower your cholesterol level and reduce the risk of heart disease, diabetes and other illnesses.

Kate Harrison is a 5:2 diet disciple – in my experience, you do get evangelical about it, particularly once you see it working – and she's written a book about it. If you're interested in finding out more, you should get it. About a week after I email her, Kate replies.

Dear Paul,

Wow, what a lovely email to get, thanks so much! Yes, I guess it does count as chick lit, though I never thought of Tracey as much of a heroine, much more a cautionary tale. I really enjoyed writing that book and going back to all my 80s memories, though I rather hated school and so it made me want to explore how it'd feel if those days had been the best of your life...

Thanks for looking beyond the girly cover, and bigger thanks for getting in touch. And glad you're finding 5:2 is working for you too, it's been such a life-changer for me!

All the best,

Kate xx

Twitter once again provides me with an interesting literary link. This time it is a podcast from *Guardian Books*, which features an interview with Richard Ford talking about *The Sportswriter*. I download it and put it on my iPod, and have a wonderful half-hour in the car listening to one of my favourite authors talking about one of my favourite books. Two things come out of this. I end up subscribing to the *Guardian Books* podcast – well, it is free – and I also decide that I will read *The Sportswriter* again. I think it might be good to read all three books in the Frank Bascombe trilogy, and from there, via a mental process I appear to have no control over or know how it works, I decide that I should have a month of reading trilogies. Indeed, I immediately designate May 'trilogy month'.

My choice of reading is to be the Bascombe books by Richard Ford, of course; Roddy Doyle's 'Last Roundup' trilogy. I've read the first book, *A Star Called Henry*, but haven't tackled its companions, even though I have two copies of the second book, *Oh Play That Thing*. I have no reasonable explanation for this state of affairs, but if you email me or contact me via social media, I will happily give you my spare copy. I also decide to tackle Cormac McCarthy's 'Border' trilogy – *All The Pretty Horses, The Crossing* and *Cities of the Plain*. I've owned a copy of *All The Pretty Horses* for years, but I've never ... well, you know the story by now.

McCarthy's stunning 2009 novel, *The Road*, is one of my favourite books which I've read several times. The first time I did so, devouring it within a couple of days and nights I was absolutely stunned by the story, the quality of the writing, the breathtaking perfection of it all. It should have pushed me towards more of his work, but somehow it didn't. I will rectify that during 'trilogy month'. Rather fortuitously, the Fopp record shop in Glasgow's West End is selling McCarthy's novels in a 'Two books for £5' offer, and I buy *The Crossing* and *Cities of the Plain*. I have all nine books now for 'trilogy month'. Yes, I'm going to attempt another nine-book month starting, on May 1, with *All The Pretty Horses*.

Before then, of course, I have to choose another book to follow *Old School Ties*, and I opt for *The Novel Bookstore* by Laurence Cosse, a French novel translated into English. I actually first spotted it in a book shop in Brooklyn during our trip to America in February. At that point, having already bought books from The Strand, I decided not to purchase Cosse's novel, although that decision only came after a long period of mental debate in the store. It's the cover which caught my eye – a couple sitting against a packed book case, both of them engrossed in a book, the image set against a blue background. I don't subscribe to the view that you should never judge a book by its cover. That's exactly what people first judge a book by. After all, more often than not, it's the front cover image, and the back cover words which prompt someone to pick it up in the first place.

I try to find out the origins of this phrase, using Google to seek the answer. 'Nothing's a mystery any more,' a friend of mine always intones, given that the correct answer to every question is just a Google search away. The downside is that people no long seem to retain the information they do find out. My enquiry reveals the following:

In 1944, the American journal 'American Speech' states 'you can't judge a book by its binding'. In 1946 the phrase first appeared in the murder mystery novel Murder in the Glass Room (by Edwin Rolfe and Lester Fuller) as 'you can never tell a book by its cover'.

However, it can be traced as far back as the first and second centuries AD, when the Roman author Juvenal wrote in Satires, 'Fronti nulla fides', which translates as, 'Never have faith in the front'.

What finally convinced me not to buy *The Novel Bookstore* in Brooklyn was the fact that a cat – a real, live cat – was sleeping on the table on top of the books. That, to me, is like someone bringing their dog into a restaurant when I'm out for a meal. I don't want to buy a book that has some cat fur thrown in for free. I'll stick to old-fashioned book marks, thank you very much. However, serendipity ensures that *The Novel Bookstore* still ends up on my shelves. I get an email from Amazon one day with recommendations for me, and Cosse's novel is among the selections. I buy it immediately.

It's an interesting book, which at first hints at being a literary crime thriller. A couple open a book shop in Paris which chooses books to stock based on their perceived literary merits rather than any commercial appeal. The books are chosen by a secret committee, and as the shop attracts praise and animosity in equal measure, several of the committee members are attacked by unknown assailants. In fact, the book is a debate on the merits of literature. What constitutes a 'good novel', and do some books deserve praise and attention over others? If so, who chooses what is considered to have a higher literary merit? While I'm reading the book, novelist Matt Haig writes a timely blog entitled 'Literary Fiction Must Go.' In it, he says:

'I hate literary fiction. Don't get me wrong, I read a lot of books that would be considered literary fiction. And I often enjoy these books. I have nothing against serious books, or intelligent books, or realistic books, or books about educated middle-class people cracking up. (I've written one or two of them myself.)

No. What I am against is the idea of literary fiction. The idea that it is – or should be – a category, a genre, something separate to, say, books about werewolves or books set in space or books revolving around love stories. And as the publishing world becomes ever more paranoid about its future there seems to be a renewed attempt to turn it into a genre of its own. This is wrong. This is dangerously wrong. I'll tell you why:

- Literary fiction is synonymous with serious fiction. By turning serious fiction into a genre you are automatically devaluing every other type of book.

- It is about snobbery. It is about that worst aspect of human nature, the one that says 'I read this type of book because I am this type of person which is a better type of person than the type who reads fantasy books/thrillers/romances/whatever'. It is book fascism.'

I recommend that you seek out the full blog. It's also only a Google click away and is well worth reading, as are many of Matt Haig's blogs. It also makes me think again of my Salman

Rushdie experience, and the fact that *The Satanic Verses* and *Midnight's Children*, both considered to be great works of literary fiction, will probably sit on my book-shelves forever without being read.

April also sees the annual Glasgow literary festival, Aye Write. I don't like the festival for personal reasons. I never get invited to take part despite being a Glasgow author with three novels published, two of which are set mainly in the city, as well as working for the biggest and most successful football club in Scotland. It's not that I haven't tried to get an invitation. I've contacted the organisers on a number of occasions, including emailing one of them after an email introduction through a writer friend which actually prompted the organiser to contact me with the words 'sounds intriguing.' Within half an hour of receiving her email, I'd replied, giving details of my books, my writing career to date and some information about myself. It was the last I heard from her. Aye Write? Aye, That'll Be Right, more like it.

So, in classic 'cutting off my nose to spite my face' style, I generally don't go to any of the Aye Write events. I know I should act my age, and as a writer who aspires to improve both personally and commercially, I should be listening to others who have already done so, but I'm very childish and immature about it all. However, I do make an exception for an event involving Tracey Thorn, the singer/songwriter most famous for being part of Everything But The Girl. She has written a memoir, *Bedsit Disco Queen: How I Grew Up And Tried To Be A Pop Star*, and, as a fan of her music, as well as having enjoyed her recent reading of the book when it was Radio 4's Book of the Week, I decide to go to the event. I even manage to 'persuade' Karen to join me, though it's only on the understanding that we go for dinner afterwards.

The event, in the main hall at the Mitchell Library in Glasgow, is packed, with over two hundred people in attendance. Most of them, I suspect, are music fans rather than literary lovers, but it's a very entertaining hour, which Karen enjoys too, though not as much as the dinner later on.

I even ask Tracey a question, something about whether part of the motivation for writing the memoir was to put it down as an historical record for her children so they can discover a side to their mother they weren't previously aware of. I don't remember the answer. I'm just relieved to have managed to get my question out without stumbling over any of the words, and making it sound sensible (I hope).

The book itself doesn't take long to read, but that's because it's well-written, entertaining and very insightful on the life of a pop star. Now emboldened after my email correspondence with Kate Harrison, I decide to 'tweet' Tracey Thorn.

@tracey_thorn Enjoyed your performance in Glasgow last Friday and enjoyed reading the book even more. Really well-written and interesting.

@PaulTheHunted Thankyou!

She replies. I have an actual genuine reply from a famous person. I am thrilled, delighted and slightly embarrassed at the same time. I'm forty-six, after all. I really do enjoy the book, and my 'tweet' to Tracey Thorn is genuine, though I'm not brave enough to dispute one passage of the book that I disagree with. Writing about her memories of the early 1980s, and how it doesn't correspond to the way the decade is remembered now in packaged nostalgia form, she says:

'It may have been Thatcher's decade, with vacuous social climbers such as Duran Duran sometimes held up to represent the whole period, but it didn't feel like that at the time. While the lovely Durannies revelled in their own dim-wittedness – There are plenty of bands catering for people who want to hear about how bad life is... We're not interested in that... One of the perks of this job is getting rich,' said Simon Le Bon – those of us who still remembered punk still held firm to the belief that the purchasing of yachts had NOT been our sole reason for deciding to form a band.

'I often feel that I barely recognise 'The 1980s' as a decade, in the form that is now remembered and repackaged for glib TV programmes. I would later see the decade reviled, and then revived, but in a manner that bore almost no relation to the years I had lived through...... Scenes which I never witnessed in my life – yuppies chugging champagne in City wine bars, toffs dancing in puffball skirts to Duran Duran – have now become the universal TV shorthand used to locate and define the era.'

I have never chugged champagne in a wine bar, anywhere. I have never bought a yacht, nor have I ever aspired to buy one, and I definitely never wore puffball skirts while dancing to Duran Duran, but I like them. I really do. I like their music. Whenever I hear the song, *Rio*, for example, it reminds me of being sixteen again, still at school, relentlessly unsuccessful with girls, but believing that life, with all of its wonderful possibilities, is going to last forever.

I have catholic tastes in music, and believe it's possible to like Everything But The Girl, Duran Duran, The Smiths, David Bowie, Girls Aloud, The Beatles, The Velvet Underground, Johnny Cash and Reo Speedwagon. This could be a playlist on my iPod. I should tell Tracey Thorn this, but I don't. I fear that we won't have a lively Twitter debate, but that she'll merely think I'm some sort of '80s yuppie throwback who's actually just a complete tosser. I'm not like that at all, and if Tracey Thorn is reading this, I hope she believes me. If she was to ever hear my version of *Rio* on the acoustic guitar, she might even change her opinion of the song … well, maybe that's going too far.

You wait ages for one memoir and then two come along at the same time. No sooner have I finished *Bedsit Disco Queen*, which has been signed by the author as well, than I start on another memoir. *Red Dust Road* by Jackie Kay is one of twenty titles selected to be given away for World Book Night. For the second year in a row I've volunteered to be a 'giver' for this event. Last year, the book I gave away was Cormac McCarthy's *The Road*, a labour of love if ever there was one, while this year it is *Red Dust Road*. I collect the books from

Bishopbriggs Library and cause a brief panic in the house when Karen fears I've bought twenty copies of the same book for some insane reason. After I've reassured her, I start reading the book.

I have a couple of tenuous connections to Jackie Kay. The first is that we were both brought up in Bishopbriggs. Her parents' house is round the corner from my old high school, and I walked past it on countless occasions, probably humming Duran Duran songs as I did so. The other link is that I once drove her home from an awards' ceremony in Edinburgh. In 2004, I was one of the prize-winners in The Scotsman/Orange short story competition with a story called *Let It Be,* and Jackie had been a guest at the event. I don't know who made the Bishopbriggs connection between us on the night, but I gave her a lift back to her mum and dad's. She won't remember, but I do. As I say, these are tenuous connections.

I want to read *Red Dust Road* ahead of World Book Night on April 24. I'm giving most of the books away at an event in a local library on the night, and I know it won't make any difference whether I've read the book or not, but I'm determined to do so, nevertheless, just in case anyone should ask me about it. It's a soft and gentle book, with Jackie's story of how she traced her birth parents running alongside the story of her own life and her relationship with her parents, the people who adopted her and brought her up. It will come as no surprise to anyone reading the book to discover that Jackie is a poet because there is a real lyricism to her narrative.

I am temporarily distracted, however, when, twenty-four hours before World Book Night, the news breaks of Reece Witherspoon's arrest in Atlanta for disorderly conduct after her husband is stopped on suspicion of drink-driving. A report on the BBC News website reveals:

Police officers stopped Ms Witherspoon and her talent agent husband James Toth after their car was spotted swerving across its lane, the online Hollywood magazine Variety reports. Citing the police report, Variety said officers breathalysed Mr Toth - the driver - whom they described as dishevelled and smelling of alcohol. During the test, Ms Witherspoon refused to heed the officer's request to stay in the car, saying she was a 'US citizen' and had a right to 'stand on American ground,' the report is quoted as saying.

'Do you know my name?' Ms Witherspoon is then reported to have asked the officer. 'You're about to find out who I am,' and 'You're about to be on national news,' she is then alleged to have said. The couple were taken into custody and later released on bail. According to the Associated Press, she released a statement on Sunday apologising for her behaviour.

'I clearly had one drink too many and I am deeply embarrassed about the things I said," she is quoted as saying, adding that: 'It was definitely a scary situation and I was frightened for my husband, but that is no excuse.'

Oh Reece, what have you done? If only we had met in The Strand that day, everything might have turned out differently.

On World Book Night, I go out to the William Patrick Library in Kirkintilloch for their annual event. I'm hoping it will be better than last year's. On a night that was supposed to be a celebration of books, the 'star' of the show was a guy singing German opera music for about an hour. I still shudder when I think about it. This year's event shows more promise – a talk by the author of an historical novel about Thomas Muir, a significant Scottish political figure with roots in the local area, along with a musical interlude by the Kirkintilloch Women's Choir. They sing a selection of show tunes, which isn't my favourite type of music, although after having to sit through what turns out to be a forty-five minute history lecture on Thomas Muir, I'm nearly on my feet and dancing when the choir start singing *'I'm Gonna Wash That Man Right Out Of My Hair'* from the musical, *South Pacific*. The talk is so long and dull that I even find myself almost hankering for some German opera music. Almost.

With 'trilogy month' less than a week away, I choose a book I'm confident of finishing ahead of May 1, and return to William McIlvanney's 1970s Glasgow and *The Papers of Tony Veitch*. It's the second of three books featuring Detective Inspector Jack Laidlaw, and the irony is not lost on me that, ahead of 'trilogy month', I'm tackling another of McIlvanney's trio of Laidlaw novels. Having enjoyed the first book, *Laidlaw*, I have high hopes for *The Papers of Tony Veitch* and the novel has the most stunning first line.

'It was Glasgow on a Friday night, the city of the stare.'

Wow! That sentence takes my breath away. There are some books you tackle like a leap in the dark, not knowing whether it will be good or not or whether you will finish it. I know, just from reading the first line, that *The Papers of Tony Veitch* is going to be a great novel and I'm going to enjoy it. I finish the book, ahead of May 1 as planned, and it confirms what I thought when I started it. It is a great novel, a classic crime thriller and a brilliant Glasgow book as well. You have to read it. I have a feeling that the third of the Laidlaw books, *Strange Loyalties*, could well be one of the first books I'll read after 'trilogy month' is over.

Three Is A Magic Number

'Reading – it's the third best thing to do in bed.'
Jarod Kintz

On Sunday, April 28, I pick up *All The Pretty Horses* and begin trilogy month. I know it's slightly cheating since I should start on the first day of May, but let's not fall out over seventy-two hours. I also have the following Tuesday off work, so it means I'm able to devote some time to Cormac McCarthy's novel. I'm intrigued to see whether my initial burst of nine books in a month was just a fluke or do I have it in me to repeat the feat. In all fairness, that was also slightly over a month, since I began on December 26 and finished on February 1, but I don't want to take too much of the shine off my achievement so I prefer to continue referring to it as 'the month of nine books.'

My first quandary is over whether to complete McCarthy's 'Border Trilogy' and then move on to Roddy Doyle before finishing with Richard Ford, or should I alternate, reading the first book in each series and then repeating the actions with books two and three … And you think you've got problems? I opt to vary the reading. It will allow the first book in each series to continue fermenting in my brain before I get to the second book, while the rotation in time and location will, hopefully, ensure that it remains interesting and never begins to feel like a chore.

There is a quote on the cover of *All The Pretty Horses* which declares it to be 'one of the best American novels of this or any other time'. That is a fairly impressive boast which any book would find difficult to live up to. My knowledge of the American novel in all its various shapes and forms is fairly limited although, off the top of my head, I can think of a handful which would probably all be jostling for that 'best

American novel' accolade. McCarthy's *The Road* and Richard Ford's *The Sportswriter* come to mind. Then there is John Steinbeck's *The Grapes of Wrath*, and *East of Eden*, Harper Lee's *To Kill A Mockingbird*, F. Scott Fitzgerald's *The Great Gatsby*, Joseph Heller's *Catch 22*, J.D. Salinger's *Catcher in the Rye*, Don DeLillo's *Underworld*, Kurt Vonnegut's *Slaughterhouse Five* and the wonderful *A Confederacy of Dunces* by John Kennedy Toole. It is, of course, an impossible task to choose, and there are probably a million and one other books I haven't mentioned, the titles of which you are now shouting out as you read this.

All The Pretty Horses might be one of those titles, and by the time May 1 comes around, I've already finished it. Is it better than *The Road*? I don't think so, but it is a stunning novel nevertheless. McCarthy has an enviable ability to implant the reader right in the heart of the story, so I can feel the Mexican dust drying my mouth, or the exhaustion of riding a horse through the country for days on end, which is particularly impressive given that I have only ever sat on a horse once in my life and that was when I was ten and my cub scout group visited the police horse stables in Glasgow. I can almost touch the scenery, sense the undercurrent of violence surging through the narrative, and taste the simmering passions of the main protagonists. As I quickly reach the end of John Grady Cole's adventures in Mexico and his return home to Texas, I'm tempted to jump straight into *The Crossing*, which is book two of the Border Trilogy, but having decided to vary authors I resist that temptation and start reading Roddy Doyle's *A Star Called Henry* instead.

I have read this book before. I thought it was brilliant the first time I did so, and a second reading of it merely confirms that initial impression. *A Star Called Henry* offers a vivid and brutal evocation of Dublin at the turn of the twentieth century. It tells the story of Henry Smart, born into a Dublin slum and left to fend for himself from a very early age. The first section of the novel deals with Henry's formative years in those slums before it moves on to 1916 and the Easter Uprising by Irish republicans. Henry is only fourteen at the time, though he claims to be older, and finds himself in Dublin's General Post Office building along with the other leaders of the 'revolution', but while his comrades are manning the barricades as the British launch their first attack on the GPO building, Henry is in the basement having sex with his former teacher.

Like so much of the novel, it casts an irreverent eye over what has become the mythology of a nation, and as I re-read the book, it makes me wonder what the reaction to *A Star Called Henry* was in Ireland when it was published. My trusty friend, Google, reveals near universal praise, which is both surprising and encouraging. Henry Smart is an 'everyman' character, always there at the important moments in Ireland's history, though he is actually nowhere, since he's a figment of Doyle's imagination. The novel reminds me occasionally of Woody Allen's film, *Zelig*, where the main character is a human chameleon, merging into the background of whatever circumstances or surroundings he finds himself in.

The copy I have is one that I purchased from Quality Paperbacks Direct, the book club I used to belong to. I had signed up after receiving one of their leaflets which promised a great introductory offer, probably something like six books for one pound, and for a couple of years I religiously ordered books, enjoying the thrill of coming home from work to find a cardboard box waiting for me to open, my enthusiasm only tempered by a dissenting voice from the shadows which would mutter darkly 'Not more bloody books!' I eventually unsubscribed, partly because my buying was far outweighing my reading, but also because they changed the concept of the club so that it was no longer just 'quality' paperbacks on offer. It was the right decision, although sometimes I still miss those cardboard boxes.

My copy also has a couple of pages which have been nibbled at the edges. I don't remember ever feeling that hungry while reading, so I know it wasn't me. In saying that, any time I've read *The Grapes of Wrath* I find that Steinbeck's description of the food gives me an urge to eat – food rather than paper, I hasten to add. Maybe someone else has borrowed the book and read it, using this method as an improvised bookmark? If so, that's just weird.

I always use a bookmark. Folding the corner of a page is a form of desecration. Eating the paper is a step beyond that. I might use an old bus ticket or a business card. I very rarely give out business cards for business reasons, but they do come in handy when I'm reading. At the moment, I'm using a proper bookmark from The Strand in New York that I got when I made a purchase there back in February. I believe, as I have done in the past, that using a certain bookmark helps in my reading, like it's bringing me luck or ensuring I keep some sort of momentum going. That's weird too, though not as weird as eating paper, obviously.

Even though I've read *The Sportswriter* several times before, it still takes longer to finish than the previous two books. It is a novel that needs to be savoured, and it retains its ability to leave me in awe of Ford's talent as a writer. I have an old battered copy which has great sentimental value, since it was the first copy I owned. It was the title which had first caught my eye, since I too am a sportswriter. I was in my mid-thirties when I first read it, so the story of Frank Bascombe, a middle-aged man in late twentieth-century America who is trying to make sense of what seems to be an increasingly unmoored and disconnected life, resonated with me, and continues to do so, though I should add that my life does not mirror Frank's, thankfully.

I have bought several copies of *The Sportswriter* over the years and passed them on to other people with an evangelical zeal. The copy I read now is a newer edition. I'm halfway through the month and I've finished three books. I realise it's unlikely that I will finish all nine books by the end of May. It's a self-imposed deadline, of course, so I can just keep going until I've successfully completed the trio of trilogies. Once again, I remind myself that this is not a race, and even if it was to take me a whole month to read a single book, then that would be fine, although secretly I would be disappointed with myself. With hindsight, I realise I should have tackled McCarthy and Doyle in their entirety, since I've read all of Ford's books before. Therefore, I decide to concentrate on them going forward.

An unexpected opportunity comes up during the month to hear William McIlvanney speaking about the *Laidlaw* books. He's giving a talk to coincide with the reissue of the trilogy. Remarkably, the books had fallen out of print, something McIlvanney mentioned at the Edinburgh Book Festival last year. It was following those comments that Edinburgh publishers Canongate stepped in to bring them back to life. Unfortunately, when I pop in to Waterstone's in Glasgow's Argyle Street ahead of the event, all the tickets have gone. Who says crime doesn't pay? Okay, so it's a free event, but it's a sign of his enduring popularity.

I leave my email address in order to receive information about future events. The following day, I get an email informing me that a ticket has been handed back and it's been put aside for me. Waterstone's have given out seventy free tickets, although it appears that only about forty people have turned up on the night. They need to introduce a better system, even if it means charging for an event. It might only be a nominal fee but that would be more liable to guarantee attendance and avoid disappointing others who might well have wanted to hear the author in question.

McIlvanney is very entertaining. He tells an interesting and appalling story of how the successful Scottish Television series *Taggart* was basically a rip-off of *Laidlaw*, instigated by someone who had been in discussions with him about the possibility of bringing his books to the TV screen. He seems sanguine about it now although I'm sure there was genuine rage at the time. The theft of intellectual property, while apparently difficult to prove in a court of law, remains a heinous one in artistic terms. I ask him a question. It seems to be what I do at author events now.

"Have you ever thought over the past few years about revisiting Laidlaw?"

There is no stuttering or stumbling on my part, and it sounds like a reasonable question in my head. McIlvanney does hint at more books, perhaps a Laidlaw prequel and then a further novel to finish off the story and the character. He's seventy-six-years-old, however, so he cautions against raised expectations lest, for whatever reason, he does not deliver.

McIlvanney is at his most eloquent, however, when he is reading, first from *Laidlaw* and then a piece of prose. The language and imagery in both is beautiful and spellbinding. In his novels, McIlvanney uses Glasgow as a distinct and important character, and his books are great in so many different ways, as Glasgow novels, Scottish novels, or as crime novels. I hope he does add to the *Laidlaw* canon. It also encourages me to think that, some thirty years younger than McIlvanney, I could be writing until I'm seventy-six. I might even write one or two decent books in that time, too.

The prose piece he reads at the end of the event, *Suffragettes for Decency*, is a short elegiac essay about his mother and her sisters, and includes a poem he wrote to her called *Visiting my Mother in my Mind in her 88th Year*, which you can read on his website.

I do not know the thoughts that come
companions to your aging,
whether your heart with grief is numb
or whether it is raging.

I wonder in your lonely nights
what old times choose to call.
Are they the ghosts of past delights?
Are they remembered gall?

And do you doubt, there in the dark,
the meaning of your life —
if it had been a wasted work,
an unrequited giving?

Listen. I have come here to say.
let all your thoughts have ease.
You've been in winter a warm day,
in choking heat cool breeze.

You've been an island in a sea,
after wild waters shore.
You've been a lesson how to be.
And no one has been more.

To hear those words read in his distinctive voice is both a poetic pleasure and a privilege. I only wish more people had been there.

Cormac McCarthy's second novel in the Border trilogy, *The Crossing*, tells the story of different characters in the same setting, and his use of language once again supplants me in that border area between the United States and Mexico of the late 1940s. In McCarthy's novels, the Mexican landscape is a character itself, similar to Glasgow in the *Laidlaw* novels. McCarthy's books are also interspersed with Spanish dialogue. My command of Spanish is 'muy pobre', but that does not detract from my enjoyment of *The Crossing*. Indeed, it feels like it's important to have included it to further enhance and authenticate the story, regardless of the fact I don't understand any of it.

The relationship that we have with other languages has long been one of distrust, disdain and dismissal. I'm talking about Scottish people here. I wouldn't claim, or want to speak for the whole of Britain, although I'm guessing it's an accusation that would easily apply throughout the island. I know, too, that it is a generalisation, and there are many Scottish people fluent in other languages. I also know people who live in Glasgow who struggle to be fluent in English, although that's another story for another day but [sic].

I once harboured a short-held ambition to speak Italian. I bought a series of CDs by Michel Thomas, popped the first one into my Walkman – that shows you how long ago it was – and sat in my room shouting out random Italian phrases in a Glaswegian accent to the bemusement and occasional alarm of my family. The experiment did not last long. Che sorpresa!

A visit to the Glasgow Film Theatre reignites my desire to become, at the very least, bi-lingual, though my language of choice this time is Hebrew; I really am that fickle. I watch *The Gatekeepers*, an Oscar-nominated documentary that tells the story of Shin Bet, the Israeli internal secret service agency, from the perspective of six former heads of the organisation. It is a fascinating film and one that I don't want to end. It offers an invaluable, and sometimes, unnerving insight into the state of Israel and the relationship it has with its neighbours, most notably the Palestinian people. I would recommend it to anyone. The film is subtitled, with all the principle characters speaking Hebrew. Their voices are captivating, telling a gripping story in a beautiful and ancient language.

The University of Glasgow, I later discover, offers beginners' classes in Hebrew. I could pretend for a couple of months that I am going to sign up for them but I know I won't. I am, I have realised, the master of instant enthusiasm but longer-term apathy. C'est la vie.

Reading Cormac McCarthy's novels also make me re-evaluate my own writing. I like to think that I can tell a story, and my own Costello Trilogy bears witness to that, *(Ed: he says modestly)* but my narrative needs more substance to elevate an interesting and entertaining story into an unforgettable one. I finish *The Crossing* on May 21 and dive head-first into Roddy Doyle's *Oh Play That Thing*. I choose one of the two hardback copies I own and discover that it's signed by the author. I remember I had gone to see Roddy Doyle in Glasgow a few years ago, but I could have sworn it was when he launched *The Woman Who Walked Into Doors*. I'm still prepared to give away a spare copy of *Oh Play That Thing*, but you're not getting my signed copy, not even if your name is 'Paul'.

Oh Play That Thing is manic, frantic and confusing, a bit like the era it's set in and I'm guessing that's deliberate from Doyle. Henry Smart has fled from the Dublin of *A Star Called Henry* to escape the death sentence imposed on him by his former IRA comrades, eventually ending up in New York of the 1920s, a time of speakeasies, jazz clubs, segregation, prohibition and gangsters. He soon finds himself on the wrong side of some of these 'wise guys', and escapes to Chicago where he ends up in tow with Louis Armstrong, the two of them at one point carrying out a series of house burglaries to get money. If it sounds a bit far-fetched, then that, unfortunately, is how it reads. I want to enjoy the book. Actually, I want to love it in the way that I love much of Doyle's work that I've read, but I feel deflated by the end, worn down by the various twists and turns in the story which, too many times, seem contrived and unconvincing. It doesn't take me long to read the book. I know I won't read it again, and if your name is 'Paul', I may well give you my signed copy now.

I'm also questioning the wisdom of Trilogy month. I've realised that part of my enjoyment in reading more this year is in not always knowing what I'm going to read next. Getting to the end of a book and then looking on my shelves to choose the next book offers a frisson of excitement and anticipation as I examine various options before choosing a particular novel. In saying that, I'm already planning my holiday reading because I'm taking my Kindle, and as I get towards the end of *Oh Play That Thing*, I'm debating whether to leave McCarthy's *Cities of the Plain* until the holiday since I've got a Kindle copy of it.

In the end I decide to complete McCarthy's Border Trilogy, as much because I fear that if I put it aside for now, I may never return to it. I'm glad that I do because *Cities of the Plain* is instantly riveting. It features the two main protagonists from the two previous books now united in this novel and is more character and plot-driven than its predecessors, although the descriptive passages remain as vivid and tangible as before. I start reading it on May 27 and finish two days later. The story is one of love and loss that is both gripping and heartbreaking. As a whole, the Border Trilogy is a paean to a world and its inhabitants that is lost forever. By the end, one of the characters, Billy Parnham, becomes a displaced wanderer, out of synch with the modern world.

Having finished McCarthy's trilogy I think, what the hell, I may as well read the final part of Doyle's trilogy too. Richard Ford's other two books will have to wait for another day. I've read them both before anyway, and I will always love the Bascombe trilogy. I know I'll return to it periodically.

The Dead Republic is better than its immediate predecessor, just, but there is a residue of dissatisfaction with the second book that I haven't quite managed to dissolve as I begin the final part of the trilogy. At the end of *Oh Play That Thing*, Henry Smart is rescued when the actor Henry Fonda stumbles upon him while urinating in the Utah desert during the filming of a John Ford film. Contrived? You better believe it. In *The Dead Republic*, Henry is returning to Ireland for the first time since the 1920s with Ford, John Wayne and Maureen O'Hara. They are meant to be filming Henry's story, with him acting behind the scenes as the 'IRA consultant', but the resultant film is actually *The Quiet Man*, a mythologised and 'Oirish' story that bears little or no resemblance to reality. It's a fine film, incidentally, and Karen and I once had our picture taken on the little bridge in Galway which is featured in the Hollywood classic.

Doyle's trilogy attempts to debunk myths of Irish republicanism, nationhood and nationality, and it features a film director coming to Ireland to capture a cinematic version of a story – facts mirroring fiction mirroring facts. What is history but one man's scripted version of it?

The Dead Republic lies somewhere between *A Star Called Henry* and *Oh Play That Thing* in terms of enjoyment. There are still too many convoluted plot twists for my liking, and I get the occasional sense that Doyle is trying to shoe-horn in a story to fit whatever themes he has determined he wants to address, or events he wants to include. It gives the whole thing an untidy feel to it, and I hate to admit that I finish the book with an overwhelming sense of relief rather than enjoyment. If it hadn't been to complete the trilogy, I would probably have abandoned *The Dead Republic* without finishing it. Actually, I wouldn't have got through *Oh Play That Thing*, never mind get on to the third book.

Cormac McCarthy's trio of books wins in a straight head-to-head with Doyle, due in no small part to what I'd perceive as a 'weakness' – a relative and subjective term, I know – of Doyle's trilogy, in particular the troublesome middle child. Maybe taking the story out of Ireland is partly to blame? Doyle is no longer in his comfort zone and the result is an uncomfortable book, although even when he does return home for the final part of the trilogy, the narrative remains disjointed and dissatisfying.

Trilogy month ends on June 4. It has lasted all of thirty-eight days, and I have managed to read seven out of the nine books. That's not a bad return. At the start of it all, my enthusiasm caused me to consider designating other months as genre-specific – crime novel month, sci-fi month, short story month, Scottish fiction month – but I have now decided to shelve that idea. The unpredictability of my reading choice is far more appealing. The highlight of this experience has been in reading Cormac McCarthy. His three novels, individually, are stunning while, collectively, I'm sure they would stand comparison with any other trilogy. They have made me re-evaluate my own writing, and where I need to improve. As for reading, I'm looking forward to a welcome change of direction.

Do Do Do Do DoDo,
Do Do Do Do DoDo

'I still love the book-ness of books, the smell of books;
I am a book fetishist. Books, to me, are the coolest
and sexiest and most wonderful things there are.'

Neil Gaiman

If you're familiar with the classic Duran Duran song *Rio* then
you may well recognise the chapter title above as the last few
lines Simon Le Bon sings as the song fades and the band, in
that classic 1980s video, sail off into the Caribbean sunset
aboard their luxury yacht. Can you hear it now? Are you
singing along to the chapter title? Good. It's worked then. If
you don't like Duran Duran, are not familiar with the song or
if you are Tracey Thorn *(see Chapter Two)*, then my efforts
have been in vain.

Having finished, not quite successfully, trilogy month, I
opt for something as far removed from Cormac McCarthy,
Roddy Doyle and Richard Ford as it's possible to be and start
reading another memoir, this time by John Taylor, bass guitar
player in Duran Duran. His book, *In The Pleasure Groove: Love,
Death and Duran Duran* tells his story from a shy, spectacled
only-child living in Birmingham to pop star pin-up, drink and
drug addict and, ultimately, to a 'clean', happily married
musician currently enjoying a resurgence in popularity along
with his fellow Duran Duran band mates.

My motivation in having bought the book is obviously my
love of the band and their music, and therein lies the
problem. As a writer, John Taylor is a great bass player. I can
tell almost immediately that a ghost writer has been involved
because it reads like a series of interviews/conversations that
have been transcribed, tidied up and presented as a

first-person narrative. A quick check of the acknowledgement page at the back of the book confirms my suspicions. The 'ghost' in question is Tom Sykes. Should I be surprised? Probably not, although I am slightly disappointed. There is a chronology to the story, with a few interesting anecdotes sprinkled throughout the book to keep readers – Duran Duran fans – happy, but the narrative lacks depth, and as I'm reading it, I have this sense of Tracey Thorn sitting behind me, legs crossed, arms folded, shaking her head and wearing a look that says 'I told you so.' I glance over my shoulder just to make sure I really am only imagining this. My opinion on the book is confirmed by a fellow Duranie (and no, that's not Cockney rhyming slang this time) in work, who had the same feelings when reading it. Yes, I also know what you're thinking. It's hard to believe there are two Duran Duran fans working at Celtic.

I have always liked Duran Duran for their music and I always will, and John Taylor has helped to write some of my favourite songs. I admire his honesty in revealing some of the excesses in his past, but I want to know more and that level of detail and revelation can only come directly through him rather than relating it to someone else. There is automatically a filter through which he relays the stories and they are then laid out on the page for him. Having previously read two books by celebrities – Molly Ringwald's novel and Tracey Thorn's memoir – both of which did not require the assistance of a ghost writer, I have to conclude that they're much better as a result. It doesn't take long to read *In The Pleasure Groove*, and while I still enjoy it, I think I'll just stick to Duran Duran's music from now on.

I choose my next book from a metaphorical blank canvas, sliding open the wardrobe doors which conceal my book collection from the world and scanning the shelves until something catches my eye. That something is *Chocolat* by Joanne Harris. It is another book which is in complete contrast to the trilogy month reading, and I realise as I start the book that the experience, particularly with Roddy Doyle's books, did have an effect on me. Having previously professed a great admiration for Doyle's work, I was taken aback by how little I enjoyed *Oh Play That Thing* and *The Dead Republic*. It seems almost sacrilegious to acknowledge that, and it feels like I have to ease myself gently back into the enjoyment of reading again after a couple of negative experiences.

The ninth of June brings the news of Iain Banks' death. It is still sudden and shocking despite his announcement at the beginning of April that he was terminally ill. While his death was inevitable and imminent, even his closest friends and family were anticipating at least another couple of months in his company. Not surprisingly, Twitter is awash with tributes. I've sometimes worried before that in similar circumstances, people are falling over themselves to post condolences or a tribute on social media like there's some sort of kudos to be attained by being the quickest to do so. I don't immediately rush to my laptop, but that same night I do 'tweet' a picture of *The Crow Road* and *The Player of Games*, my favourite books by Iain Banks and Iain M. Banks.

In this instance, I can see the appeal and positive aspects of social media. A disparate 'community' of readers and writers who have read Iain (M) Banks' novels have been brought together through Twitter and are able to acknowledge how much they enjoyed the books and how desperately sad it is that a fifty-nine-year-old man has died. Most of us never knew Iain Banks, but through his books we believe we did, and that is a legacy very few writers ever manage to achieve. The words of the Argentinian writer, Jorge Luis Borges seem apt.

'When writers die they become books which is, after all, not too bad an incarnation.'

Banks' death makes me think of my own mortality. I will be forty-seven this year. I'm getting old. I still feel young, and participate in sports – mainly five-a-side football and badminton – as if I am young. I know I'm not. Occasionally,

I'll study my face in the mirror, slightly puzzled. Who is this middle-aged bald man with a greying beard staring back at me? He looks a little like my dad, or so people often tell me. I study my dad sometimes now, seeing myself as I'll be when I'm even older, in my seventies. I've already told Karen what I want for my seventieth birthday – a packet of cigarettes and a *Playboy*. I figure that if I make it to seventy, then taking up smoking again won't make much difference; I say this without any medical evidence to back it up, and even as I write this, I realise it actually sounds idiotic. The *Playboy* is self-explanatory, though it may well be that by the time I get to that age, I will only be reading it for the articles.

My ambitions – the ones that aren't fatuous or facile, like learning to drive a bus so that I can go on a trip across Europe á la Cliff Richard in *Summer Holiday* – remain much the same now at the age of forty-six as they were when I was sixteen, and which I guess will remain the same until I'm that puffing pensioner with a penchant for pornography. I wanted to be a writer – a novelist – since I was very young and I have achieved that. I've managed to write three novels that have been published. Not too many people have bought or read them, but that's another, more frustrating story. I'd like to be a best-selling novelist, but that success has so far eluded me. There is still time, of course. I may consider myself to be getting old. I am. We all are. But I'm 'only forty-six,' as people sometimes remind me, so there is plenty of time yet.

I love reading books and I've read a lot already this year, much more than I have done in previous years. I've enjoyed most of them. I like to think that I read good books, in that there is some literary merit to them. I need to write books like that too.

The BBC broadcasts an interview that Iain Banks gave to Kirsty Wark shortly before his death. It is moving, entertaining, captivating and, ultimately, very sad. Around the same time another Scottish writer dies. Frederic Lindsay, the author of several thrillers, passes away at the age of seventy-nine. It's not as big a shock as Iain Banks' death, given that Lindsay is older and not as well-known, but his death makes me think of his first novel, *Brond*, which I read many years ago on the back of Channel 4's adaptation. It's a strange and unusual crime story, which was reflected in the TV series, both of which were enjoyable; I don't need to tell you which I preferred. The TV version featured a very young John Hannah in the title role, whose acting talents, I have to admit, continue to pass me by, although he does get plenty of big roles, so maybe it is just me, while his voice appears to appeal to advertisers looking for an actor to do voiceover work for their products, such as Direct Line Insurance or the Co-op supermarket – 'Good with food.'

Reading *Chocolat,* it would be a bit obvious to admit that it's a delicious read, but it really is. Did you like that seamless link between Co-op food and *Chocolat?* The book is a magical, fantastical, bewitching love story, and I finish it within a couple of days. The same night I finish the book, I watch the film adaptation, which I have had stored on Sky+ for a few months. It provides the perfect opportunity to compare the book to the film. Joanne Harris' book wins hands down. If you've tasted both, so to speak, then you will undoubtedly agree. The book is wonderful, and I find myself craving chocolate – so much for the 5:2 Diet. The film is okay. It has the usual changes to the storyline which Hollywood often demands, sometimes in order to squeeze a long story into a ninety-minute film, but sometimes for inexplicable reasons, such as Johnny Depp with an Irish accent. In the film's defence, it does star Juliette Binoche. Enough said.

I didn't realise there was a sequel to *Chocolat* until a colleague at work mentions it, along with a promise to lend me it. It's next on my list to read after I decide to tackle a James Kelman novel. Kelman is considered to be one of Scotland's greatest ever novelists, but I have struggled in the past with his work. Memories of my Salman Rushdie experience lurk in the background, but I decide to persevere anyway, hoping that in tackling *You Have To Be Careful In The Land Of The Free*, I will have a Kelman-breakthrough.

I have a signed copy from 2004, when I had gone through to the Edinburgh Book Festival to hear him reading. The inscription reads *'For Paul from James Kelman. 25/8/04'*. It does strike me as funny that I've gone from reading *Chocolat* to *How To Be Careful In The Land Of The Free,* which is either from the sublime to the ridiculous, or vice-versa, depending on your point of view. I'm not sure James Kelman would approve.

In an ideal world, I would read Kelman's novel in one sitting, since it is a stream of consciousness narrative taking place over a few hours. I can immediately appreciate the absolute skill involved in being able to tell a story in that style and, more importantly, keep the reader (me) engaged. Kelman's novel is superb, absolutely captivating in its detail and very thought-provoking. It's worth noting, given that it was written in 2004, how prescient it is now, nine years later, with America's ongoing 'war on terror', an alarming increase in surveillance, both domestic and international, as well as an upsurge in general suspicion of the 'stranger' in our midst. Unfortunately, like many things which happen in the United States, this is mirrored in Britain. Kelman wrote a prophetic novel, which is both admirable and chilling.

At this time, news is leaked by a former CIA employee, Edward Snowden, that the American government has been spying on Internet companies and, specifically, their users – that's you and me, folks – apparently prompting an upsurge in the number of people buying and reading George Orwell's *1984.* I read it again a few years ago, realising that the 'war on terror' was classic Orwellian double-speak, and what the United States and Britain have been doing the past few years is exactly what Orwell describes in *1984,* even if his original warnings were in relation to the former Soviet Union. Everyone should read it, and then be very scared. They should read Kelman's novel as well.

I struggled before with James Kelman, but maybe getting back into the reading habit has cleared my mind and enabled me to tackle something that I would have previously shied away from? Whatever the reason, I'm glad, because *You Have To Be Careful In The Land Of The Free* is a masterful novel. However, I'm still not going to read Salman Rushdie, not even if you try and make me.

As well as reading more books this year – my current total after Kelman currently stands at thirty-six – I've found that I have also been buying more books. That is the 'downside' of reading more, if you can call it that. That's what Karen would call it if you asked her. So don't ask her. I've rediscovered a love of buying books, due in part because I've managed to shrug off the inevitable guilt I used to feel, knowing that my purchases would join many others on my shelves, there to remain untouched and unread. Now, I have a sense of purpose and if the books are not read immediately, then I feel they won't be left on the shelf for months or years, or at least I hope most of them won't be. Alfred Edward Newton was an American author, publisher, and avid book collector who, at the time of his death in 1940, had an estimated ten thousand books in his collection. He once wrote:

'The buying of more books than one can read is nothing less than the soul reaching towards infinity, and this passion is the only thing that raises us above the beasts that perish.'

If it's any consolation to Karen, I don't have nearly as many books as Newton, although I've resisted cataloguing my own collection in case the actual figure still scares and/or appals her. I have always loved buying books, almost as much as I've loved reading them, though over the past few months I've noticed my book-buying habits changing. Nowadays, the centre of Glasgow only really has two bookshops of note to boast of – both of them Waterstone's (I'm still using the apostrophe, incidentally, because it's the right thing to do). When I go into either of the stores now, what strikes me about them is their sparseness, like they're under-stocked or being run-down with a view to closing them. I remember years gone by, when I was a daily visitor to the now-deceased

Waterstone's at the corner of Union Street and Gordon Street in the city, that it seemed like there weren't enough shelves for all the stock, and there would be piles on the floor that you sometimes had to step over or round like navigating a crudely-assembled obstacle course.

The 'High Street' is a difficult place for bookshops, and many have disappeared from our landscape; I fear that one day, in the not too distant future, they will be gone completely. There are a number of reasons for this and I am as culpable as the next reader of heralding their decline if not demise. I buy a lot of books online now, whether from Amazon or second-hand from one of the many sellers using Amazon as a platform. I buy books from supermarkets such as ASDA or Tesco, with their 'Two Books for £7' or 'Three Books for £10' offers. I also visit the Oxfam charity shop in Bishopbriggs. My motivation has little to do with charity but more because the paperbacks are on sale for just £1.99. Indeed, one of my (fatuous) ambitions is to walk in one day and see a copy of one of my novels on sale in the Oxfam shop. I don't know if that means I will have 'made it', but at least it will indicate that enough of my books are in circulation for people to be donating them to charity shops.

I should buy my books from Waterstone's, or find another retailer to patronise. It's the 'right' thing to do, for the future of the publishing industry and for the benefit of my fellow authors too. It will be a sad day if, or when, there are no book shops left in our cities. I suspect that independent book shops will continue to exist and even thrive, though away from any metropolis and its exorbitant or prohibitive rents.

Having finished James Kelman, I return to Joanne Harris and *The Lollipop Shoes*, her sequel to *Chocolat*. There is an eight-year gap between the books, and the sequel is nowhere near as good. It feels bloated and over-written, like it was a second or third draft that needed a further forensic edit, and I find myself skim-reading it in order to finish it, with relief. I actually should give up on it, but I persevere until the bitter end. Thankfully it hasn't managed to put me off chocolate.

It's fast approaching June 29 when I'm heading off on holiday, a seventeen-day break that involves three days in Santa Ponsa, a week's cruise in the Mediterranean, followed by another week in Santa Ponsa. I've packed the Kindle full of reading material, so rather than start a novel which I might have to leave behind to pick up again in the middle of July, I decide to dip into some of the short story collections I have. I've started writing some short stories again, so I figure it will be good 'research' to help in my own writing.

I've often presumed, erroneously as it turns out, that in this age of instant information and instantly disposable culture, people would read short stories since they seem, on the surface, to fit in with the pace of modern life and the apparent lack of time everyone seems to have these days. One of my favourite films is *Ferris Bueller's Day Off*, and one of the most memorable lines is when Ferris, in justifying faking illness to have a day off school, says, 'Life moves pretty fast. If you don't stop and look around once in a while, you could miss it.' It is a great line, and wise advice. It was when the film was released in 1986 and it's even more pertinent now.

However, it does appear that people don't read short stories, which is a great pity, since there are some wonderful stories and writers out there whose work deserves a wider audience. I've always felt that a suspicion, ignorance or avoidance of short stories is more prevalent on this island. America seems to have a greater appreciation of the form, and a more established tradition, certainly throughout the twentieth century and into the new Millennium. Joyce M. Reid, who edited the *Classic Scottish Short Stories* anthology back in 1990, wrote in her introduction to the collection:

'A short story should be something between a poem and a reflection, a novel and an anecdote. The very best stories have a little of the character of all four.'

I decide to start with an anthology of short stories featuring the best stories from The Scotsman & Orange Short

Story Award 2004. By a strange coincidence (or not!), the book features my story, *Let It Be*, which was one of the prize-winning stories. I also note that the anthology was actually edited by Jackie Kay, which I'd forgotten about. My connection, through growing up in the same town and me having given her a lift home from Edinburgh, extends to her having selected my story as one of the best in this competition. In her introduction she writes of my short story:

'Let It Be tells the story of a prostitute taking her mind off the job, as it were, by immersing herself in Beatles' songs. There is an appealing redemptive wit in this story. Michelle is trapped in a car, just as the central character in 'Masonry' (the winning story) is clinging to a wall. The short story is such a pure and distilled form that it can brave moments of anguish or shame or anger and stay there. We can take it in a short story; sip it neat like a nippy malt... What is exciting about these stories is how totally different they are from each other, how each writer has a unique and particular voice.'

I also note that in the short biographical paragraph at the back of the book that *'Paul Cuddihy . . . is currently working on his first novel.'* It only took another six years until *Saints and Sinners* actually came out, though I wasn't working on that particular novel in 2004.

My story is written in the Glaswegian vernacular, and I've often wondered if that was the reason it didn't actually win the competition, which would have meant the difference between a five-hundred pound cheque and one for three thousand pounds. I really enjoy the story. (*It's very good, he says modestly*). I actually wrote another short story, *Ticket To Ride*, which featured the same character and which ended up being selected for inclusion in the anthology of another competition. On the back of that I began writing a novel, also called *Let It Be*, and managed to produce about twenty-five thousand words before I ran out of steam. I don't know if I was convinced a novel so broadly and blatantly Glaswegian would have much appeal beyond the city's boundaries, but it's something that remains in my drawer, patiently waiting for me to take it out and have a look at it again at some point.

My original intention is to dip in and out of the short story collections I own, sampling individual stories by various writers. I realise, however, that this is only liable to create a literary leaning tower of Pisa at the side of my bed and so instead I opt for one collection, *When The Women Come Out To Dance* by Elmore Leonard.

The stories, not surprisingly, are great; little vignettes of lives on either side of the law. The first one I read is *Karen Makes Out*, a funny and absorbing tale of an American law enforcement officer who ends up having an affair with a suspected bank robber who is being tracked by the FBI. Like all of Leonard's work, the language is precise, with not a word out of place. It's a short story, but I'm immediately immersed in the world he has created, and the conclusion lingers long in the memory, which can also be said of the rest of the stories in the collection.

Anyone interested in becoming a writer, or indeed, anyone who is already a writer should read Elmore Leonard's '10 Rules of Writing'. They are witty and wise, and anyone would do well to follow them. Of course, you could always check out my website and an article I wrote offering my own rules of writing. Elmore Leonard's are better, of course, although some of mine might be funnier.

The month ends with the suitcase packed for the holiday and my oldest daughter, Louise telling me that she's finally finished my second novel, *The Hunted*, which she read when she was on holiday in Tunisia. She enjoyed it – well, she's got to say that, hasn't she – and she's now got the third book in the trilogy, *Land Beyond The Wave*, to read, while I've got seventeen Internet-free days to immerse myself in books, in between all the eating and drinking that has to be done. It's a hard life.

Lazing On A Sunny Afternoon

'Books are no more threatened by Kindle than stairs by elevators.'
Stephen Fry

This month, I've chosen a more familiar song for a chapter heading, which should certainly resonate with readers of a certain vintage. It is, of course, a line from the classic Kinks song, an appropriate choice on two counts. Firstly, it sets the scene for the fact much of my reading over the next three weeks will be as I laze under the Mediterranean sun, and secondly, *Sunny Afternoon* is the song that was Number One in the British charts back on July 15, 1966 when I was born. While there was obviously nothing I could do to influence what was the pick of the pops back in the sixties, it has always been a relief that my 'birth song' is a great one.

We leave for Majorca on June 29, flying out from Prestwick Airport. My Kindle is loaded and ready to use, with one hundred and forty-eight books now in the palm of my hand as I sit waiting for that awful moment when the plane accelerates down the runway, having been given the green light to take off. At this point, Kindles and other such devices have to be switched off, although since my eyes are shut and my hands are clasped together in fervent prayer, there's no way I'd be reading even if the pilot let me.

Once the 'seatbelt' sign has been switched off, which means we're probably about thirty-thousand feet in the air – let's not think about that any more – I switch on the Kindle. My holiday reading begins with *The 100-year-old Man Who Climbed Out Of A Window And Disappeared* by Jonas Jonasson. The title of the book offers the perfect summary of the plot, and it reminds me of a number of different things as I'm reading it; there are shades of P.G. Wodehouse in the 'farce' of the story – a 100-year-old man, a suitcase of money, bungling criminals and an elephant, amongst other elements. The author explains in an interview printed at the back of the book that he always wanted to write a story with that title and, to be fair, it is a great title. I'm terrible with titles; some people might argue that I'm terrible with the rest of the words too, but I'll just ignore them.

The main protagonist of the book, Allan Karllsom, also recounts in the course of his adventure the story of his life and his connections to some of the major events and figures of the twentieth century. It's another book which reminds me of Woody Allen's film, *Zelig*, or even Henry Smart in Roddy Doyle's *Last Roundup* trilogy, where history is seen through the eyes of an 'ordinary' observer, and it poses the question of who writes our history and whether the 'ordinary' man is always erased; maybe it's all made up? That element of the book does become slightly tiresome and contrived after a while, although the main narrative of the centenarian's adventures remain entertaining enough to compensate.

Next up is *Disgrace* by J.M. Coetzee, a powerful novel of post-apartheid South Africa. As I'm reading this, the news comes out of South Africa that Nelson Mandela, the former ANC leader and 'father of the nation' is critically ill in hospital. Coetzee's novel, which won the Booker Prize back in 1999 – one of only a handful of Booker Prize-winning novels that I've ever managed to read – has so many different strands running through it. It's a story of scandal, of a battle of the sexes, as well as a battle of the races, between the old and new South Africa. It could easily have descended into a novel of titillation about the brief affair between an older man and a much younger woman, but Coetzee handles the subject matter with great skill and care, and it leaves a strong impression long after I've finished it. I'll also be able to watch the film now, which I recorded on Sky+ earlier in the year for Rebecca because she was studying the book at university.

I've always been curious as to what other people read, and being on holiday usually allows a glimpse into the reading habits of my fellow sun-worshippers. People read more on holiday. I'm sure that, for some people, it's the only time of the year they pick up a book. I try not to pass judgement on anyone's reading choices, not even the year when every second person seemed to be reading the autobiography of Katie Price (Jordan). Okay, so maybe I did sit at the hotel pool thinking that I was better than everyone who was reading that book but I never said it out loud, and that's got to count for something.

This year I spot a couple of people reading former Manchester United player, Gary Neville's autobiography, while there is a smattering of crime novels and 'chick-lit' books – the pastel colours are a giveaway – but it's more difficult now because of the increase in electronic devices – mainly Kindles and iPads – so people could be reading anything – porn ... sorry, erotic fiction, Mills & Boon, maybe even a Katie Price novel, which is surely an oxymoron! In a *Daily Telegraph* column, literary critic Tom Payne offers an interesting perspective on why we read on holiday, beginning with a short, but fascinating, history lesson.

'We are evolving into a species that reads on holiday. We want to travel light, but to expand our minds. It has taken us years to reach a point at which we can do it well. As with so many advances in civilisation, the Romans had almost achieved what we have, only for their progress to be eclipsed by the Dark Ages. They had travel scrolls, and Martial mentions that huntsmen would pack them into string bags. Scrolls were tricky to read anywhere except at home, preferably at a table, but at least our forebears tried. These matters became easier with the invention of codices, which had pages. By the sixth century, Saint Benedict of Nursia could prescribe that his order of monks took a book with them whenever they went on a journey. Some scholars went to great lengths to make literature portable: Abdul Kassem Ismael, the 10th-century Grand Vizier of Persia, travelled with 400 camels following him, each in alphabetical order, to bear his library of 117,000 books.'

While I often marvel at the wonders of twenty-first century technology that allows me to carry hundreds of books in my right hand and thousands of songs in my left, it suddenly seems less impressive compared to Abdul Kassem Ismael and his four hundred camels trudging through the desert in alphabetical order ... and he needed more camels since the Persian alphabet has thirty-two letters. Apparently the Grand Vizier was such an avid reader that he couldn't bear to leave home without all his books – I know the feeling – although it must have been a nightmare finding all those grains of sand between the pages. Tom Payne goes on to say:

For holiday reading, there are really three choices. There are books you want to be seen reading; there are books you want to have read; and there are the books you want to read. I asked people who were stuck at Bristol Airport how they felt about this issue, and met a sales rep who had taken Noam Chomsky's 'Monkeywrenching the New World Order' on his last excursion, then read his girlfriend's copy of 'The Great Gatsby'. Next holiday he's taking the new Harry Potter. These represent all three options: the brainy thesis, the artful classic, and the undemanding page-turner.

The hero of Anne Tyler's 'The Accidental Tourist' falls into the first category. Macon Leary writes guides for business travellers who don't really want to explore the countries they visit, and advises: 'Always bring a book, as protection against strangers. Magazines don't last. Newspapers from home will make you homesick, and newspapers from elsewhere will remind you that you don't belong.' The book he carries is Miss MacIntosh, My Darling, by Marguerite Young. It weighs in at 1,198 pages. Leary is a character who believes in saving energy, so his holiday reading is admirably efficient. Like Philip Swallow (character in David Lodge's novel Small World), he manages to take it everywhere, and although he is engrossed in it, he doesn't get through it. 'Any time he raised his eyes, he was careful to mark a paragraph with his finger and to keep a bemused expression on his face.'

I'm glad that Payne mentions Anne Tyler because it's a good excuse to extol the virtues of one of the finest novelists around. I've read *The Accidental Tourist*, and many of her other novels besides. In fact, I have thirteen Anne Tyler novels, more than just about any other writer, apart from Roddy Doyle. Tyler's novels are all set in her native Baltimore and while they might seem, at first glance, to be ordinary tales of ordinary people, she tells their stories in such a profound and poetic way that every novel is actually an extraordinary experience. I'd like to say that I aspire to write like Anne Tyler, but who am I kidding? Just go out and get one of her books – after reading this one, of course – and see for yourself. You won't be disappointed.

I take a trip back to my adolescence with my next book, Len Deighton's *SS-GB*. The premise of the book is that Germany won the Second World War and Britain is under Nazi occupation. I was fourteen or fifteen when I first read the book, and at the time I was enthralled. While it is enjoyable enough to re-read, I'm never going to be able to recapture that initial teenage excitement or, indeed, transport myself back to a time of innocence, optimism and endless opportunities. I don't know if that's what I hoped for when I started reading it but, if so, it's a naïve and forlorn hope. If you want to read something along a similar theme, you'd be better checking out Robert Harris' *Fatherland*. I read that novel over twenty years ago when it came out in 1992 and I read it again last year. It remains a brilliant story.

From a fictional account of 1940s Britain under German occupation, I travel back to seventeenth century Germany and another book in Oliver Potzsch's 'Hangman's Daughter' series, involving an executioner and torturer in Bavaria, Jakob Kuisl. I read the first book, called *The Hangman's Daughter*, thirty-thousand feet in the air on a plane to New York. I read *The Beggar King* on a cruise ship in the middle of the Mediterranean Sea. I'd actually chosen it thinking it was the second book in the series, though I subsequently discover that it's actually number three. I don't think it lessened any enjoyment of *The Beggar King*, and this book is as thrilling and well-written as the series opener. The historical detail is brilliant and you really feel transported back to seventeenth century Bavaria. It's a book I can't put down, well, until the battery dies on the Kindle one night and I have to wait until it's re-charged the following day to finish it. I will definitely have to read *The Dark Monk*, which is the actual second book in the series, though I'll possibly have to arrange another holiday to accompany it, just to remain consistent.

I've discovered that sometimes it's easier to read a book on Kindle than the actual physical copy. When I say 'easier', I mean less daunting. I presume there must be an element of perception, because apart from the bar at the bottom of the Kindle screen informing me what percentage of the book I've read, there is no sense of the size or scale of any e-book I'm reading. It also feels, with the constant 'turning' of the page, that I'm progressing more quickly and steadily through a book. There may well already be studies on the psychology of reading e-books compared to actual ones. If not, some group of boffins will probably apply for, and receive, a six-figure grant to 'study' the subject and come up with 'answers' that common sense and an hour chatting with readers would provide just as easily and more cheaply.

Nevertheless, I certainly find it easier to read *One Hundred Years of Solitude* by Gabriel Garcia Marquez. I'd tried reading it before but gave up. This time I devour it quickly. It's a fantastic, fantasy-riddled, passionate, bizarre tale of a Latin American village whose history has already been written by a gypsy, and lives are spent trying to decipher what has been transcribed. It poses questions of what is truth, myth, fiction, fact or fable, similar in many ways to *The 100-year-old Man Who Climbed Out Of A Window And Disappeared*. Marquez's *One Hundred Years of Solitude* is a magical book and in this instance I'm grateful for the advent of the e-reader.

Christopher Brookmyre is one of Scotland's most successful novelists, who also has a fine line in great book titles – *A Big Boy Did It And Ran Away*, *Be My Enemy (Or Fuck This For A Game Of Soldiers)*, *The Attack of the Unsinkable Rubber Ducks*, and *All Fun And Games Until Somebody Loses An Eye*, to name but four – but I have to confess than I have never read any of his books. I did once have some contact with him a few years ago when the *Celtic View* magazine wanted to publish his masterful feature *'Playground Football'*. He gave us permission, his only stipulation being that we had to stress that he was, and is, a St Mirren supporter. If you want to read *Playground Football* – and I urge you to do so – you can find it on the author's website. If you have ever kicked a ball in earnest in a school playground, you will love it.

Having finished with Gabriel Garcia Marquez, I decide to tackle my first Brookmyre novel, and opt for *Pandaemonium*. It's a story of teenagers on a school trip, secret military activity in the Scottish mountains, demons from another planet and the power and influence of the Catholic Church. Some of the novel is outrageously hilarious – the bus scene with the pupils on the way to an outdoor centre is laugh-out-loud funny, and the whole novel offers a brilliant portrayal of teenagers. There are also a number of targets Brookmyre chooses to mock, including organised religion, and the Catholic Church in particular, and even Dan Brown's *Da Vinci Code* novel. As I read the book, it does make me think of *Lost*, the American TV series where a plane crashes on a deserted island and it takes six series and one hundred and twenty-one episodes to discover that all the 'survivors' of the crash are, in fact, dead. I wonder whether the characters in Brookmyre's *Pandaemonium* all died in the bus crash at the start of the book and the rest of the novel is the product of dead teenagers' imaginations.

The holiday is slowly drawing to a close and after sailing round the Mediterranean, we've taken up temporary residence in Santa Ponsa on the island of Majorca. On July 15, I celebrate my forty-seventh birthday, and as in previous years, I mark the occasion with a lot of alcohol in an Irish pub, which includes me getting up to play the guitar and sing something by The Beatles or Oasis. It's only because I can remember the words to their songs although back in 2010, the night Spain won the World Cup, I had celebrated the triumph as if my name was Pablo. Later, I made the mistake of getting up to sing, and while I could remember the chords of various songs, I lost the power of speech and was reduced to emitting a few tuneless noises, much to the amusement of my wife and friends.

Birthdays don't really make me melancholic, though each one is a reminder that time is running out if I want to achieve the things I've always wanted to do – write books for a living, mainly, along with learning to drive that double-decker bus. I realise there's no point in making any new resolutions about my life, certainly not while I'm on holiday, and I always tend to count my blessings for what I have rather than bemoan anything I don't… as well as gazing wistfully at passing buses.

My seventh book turns out to be my second Booker Prize winner of the summer – Hilary Mantel's *Wolf Hall*. It's a first-class historical novel, set in sixteenth-century England, which tells the fictional story of Thomas Cromwell's rise in the court of Henry VIII. The novel is set during an important time in history, when the church and crown in England split from the Church of Rome because the king wanted a son and needed a new wife to provide him with one. It also illustrates the importance of the invention of the printing press to the success of the Reformation, not only in spreading Martin Luther's *95 Theses* throughout Europe, but also in producing 'banned' copies of the Bible in the language of different countries that spread the protestant word of God. The detail in *Wolf Hall* is superb, while the characterisation makes for a fascinating and captivating book. It's no surprise that it has garnered much praise and many awards. It's also a mark of Mantel's talent that *Bring Out The Bodies*, the sequel to *Wolf Hall*, also won the Booker Prize, in 2012. It's now on my 'books to read' list.

Like all good things, the holiday eventually draws to an end, although like all previous holidays, it does get to the point where I'm pleased to get home – to my own house, my own bed, my acoustic guitar … and I return to physical books, packing my Kindle away for the next, as yet unplanned, holiday and picking up *The Yellow Birds* by Kevin Powers. I'm immediately reminded just how much I love books. I've read seven e-books, and enjoyed them all but it only serves to reinforce the gulf between the physical and the virtual.

Books are one of humanity's greatest ever inventions, and the prototype has remained relatively untouched over the centuries. The covers – the best of them – can be works of art, as can the actual lay-out inside. In some respects, and this again might be an age thing, it's like comparing vinyl LPs to CDs, or worse, digital downloads. Album covers back in the day were memorable works of art. Who even cares or knows what an album cover looks like now? I fear the same may become true of books. Author Ray Bradbury, who died in 2012 at the age of ninety-one, once said:

'I still love books. Nothing a computer can do can compare to a book. You can't really put a book on the Internet. Three companies have offered to put books by me on the Net, and I said, 'If you can make something that has a nice jacket, nice paper with that nice smell, then we'll talk.' All the computer can give you is a manuscript. People don't want to read manuscripts. They want to read books. Books smell good. They look good. You can press it to your bosom. You can carry it in your pocket.'

It's not that I've suddenly discovered something I didn't already know, but it's nice to be reminded. I feel like I should remind you too, though I suspect I'm preaching to the converted. I also have to keep reminding myself as I'm writing this that I'm planning to release this book myself in an electronic format, as well as a physical product, having accepted, almost fatalistically, that no publisher would be interested in my words. Yes, I am a book-loving hypocrite.

The Yellow Birds by Kevin Powers is one of the first novels to have come out of the most recent war in Iraq. The author fought with the US Army in the conflict, and the novel is a powerful account of someone suffering post-traumatic stress disorder. As a writer, I am always slightly jealous – and when I say 'slightly', I mean minutely so – of other writers living in conflict zones, because it gives them a ready-made supply of material for their writing, so expect a raft of Syrian-based novels in the next two or three years. However, I do realise that there are a few challenges to living in such places, staying alive being the main one.

Towards the end of the month, there is a Twitter storm regarding the announcement that Jane Austen's image is going appear on a Bank of England ten-pound note from 2017 onwards. The decision follows an online petition organised by a blogger, Caroline Criado-Perez, which claims discrimination by the Bank because there are no women on their notes, apart from the Queen. The newly-appointed governor of the Bank of England, Mark Cairney, explains: 'Jane Austen certainly merits a place in the select group of historical figures to appear on our banknotes. Her novels have an enduring and universal appeal and she is recognised as one of the greatest writers in English literature.'

Given that I read *Pride ana Prejudice* earlier in the year, I can testify to the novel's 'enduring and universal appeal'. I have to admit I'm nonplussed as to whether or not Jane Austen appears on a ten-pound note. If I'm being honest I hope that, by 2017, Scotland will be an independent country and a Bank of England ten-pound note, with or without Austen's image, will be foreign currency. I actually wrote a poem about the problems Scottish people sometimes encounter when trying to buy something in England. It's called *Foreign Exchange*.

Huv ye goat change ae a tenner?
Ah asked the wumin.
She looked at me kinda funny,
like a wis talkin
another language,
so ah asked her again, slowly,
l-i-k-e s-h-e w-i-s a-n i-d-i-o-t
an she understood,
but when ah haunded her the note,
she telt me she didnae take Scottish money.

I would have forgotten all about the issue if there hadn't been an outpouring of misogynistic rage, primarily directed towards Caroline Criado-Perez, but also to some female MPs who supported her campaign. Rape and death threats led to it becoming a police matter. It's a depressing, if familiar development. The anonymity of social media allows such venom to exist.

There was recently a warning issued by the head of Saudi Arabia's religious police against using Twitter. No, honestly, there really was. Sheikh Abdul Latif Abdul Aziz al-Sheikh said anyone using social media sites – and especially Twitter – 'has lost this world and his afterlife'. Twitter is the platform for those who do not have any platform, he said. There is a tiny part of me and maybe part of you too, which agrees with Sheikh Abdul Latif Abdul Aziz al-Sheikh, at least up to a point, though given that in Saudi Arabia, women aren't even allowed to drive, it might be slightly disingenuous, if not wholly inappropriate, to use the Sheikh's warning about Twitter in relation to a misogynistic tsunami of abuse on the social media platform.

The Sheikh's negativity, and mine too, could be because of Twitter's vacuous soul, its glorification of the banal, its ability to foster and fester hate, or its contribution to the destruction of the English language – that one's just my gripe. Okay, so I've repeated these criticisms before. I'll quit while I'm behind and go away to fine-tune my online marketing strategy for this e-book. LOL!

#Curmudgeon

'I would be most content if my children grew up to be the kind of people who think decorating consists mostly of building enough bookshelves.'

Anna Quindlen

Okay, so hands up who has forgotten my warning about using 'LOL' or any other annoying twenty-first century acronyms such as 'LMAO', 'LMFAO' or 'PMSL'. I was just being sarcastic at the end of the previous chapter. I hope you realised that. I'm a hypocrite about many things, but definitely not that.

If July ends with another Twitter rant, then August begins with another example of how social media can actually work well for books. John Williams' novel, *Stoner*, is being promoted as a forgotten classic of American literature. Much of the online hype is being led by the publishers, Vintage Classics, and in my weakness I'm seduced, so much so that I buy the book. It tells the story of William Stoner, who spends his entire adult life in the same university, having enrolled as a student at the age of nineteen and never left. His is an unhappy and unfulfilled life, having married the wrong woman, and I find myself occasionally infuriated by him, wishing I could dive into the book, grab him by the jacket lapels and scream into his face, 'Pull yourself together! Dump her and get on with your life!' I enjoy the book but I'm not convinced it lives up to the onslaught of social media praise it has garnered. I wonder, too, if the novel has been, over the years, slightly misleading or disappointing to readers, particularly in the United States, who might have picked it up thinking that *Stoner* was actually a novel about drugs and felt cheated when it transpired it wasn't.

I progress on to *The Knot* by Mark Watson, and start

reading it with a slight degree of trepidation, which is a strange way to approach any book. My reluctance stems from the fact that the author is a 'celebrity' – he's a well-known comedian who often pops up on my telly and yours too – and I have a general disdain for such people who have 'written' books, such as celebrity biographies, novels or party-planning tomes. I should state for the record that Mark Watson, thankfully, does not fall into this category. For one thing, he writes his own novels, and *The Knot* is a fine work of fiction. It tells the story of a wedding photographer's life, the premise being, at least from the synopsis on the back cover, that the photographer has spent his career capturing other people's 'special day' while always remaining an outside observer and never being the centre of attention on his own wedding day. I was actually expecting it to be a light-hearted romance in the style of *Four Weddings and a Funeral*, though thankfully without Hugh Grant, but while it is entertaining and funny too – not surprisingly – it's also quite disturbing and a lot darker than I had anticipated. I am impressed enough to take to Twitter to tell the author.

I write: '*@watsoncomedian Just wanted to say how impressed I was by The Knot. Deceptively serious and startling at times … and quite funny too.*'
His reply, to me and another tweeter who has complimented him at the same time, reads: '*@lauralaverick @PaulTheHunted This pair of tweets brightened my day up no end. Thanks.*'

And so another celebrity connection is born…
The Edinburgh International Book Festival kicks off on August 9 and it virtually passes me by. It's on for fourteen days and not one of those days finds me in the Scottish capital. I could pretend that it's because I can't get any time off work, and there's an element of truth in that, given I've not long returned after a three-week holiday. However, there's also a suspicion of all things Edinburgh that is peculiar

to Glasgow. It's hard to explain this to non-Glaswegians, but for many of us, it does lead to a reluctance to have anything to do with our east coast neighbours, even though there's a distance of less than fifty miles separating both cities. We tend to think we're better, kinder and funnier than Edinburghians, a sort of inverse snobbery. Glaswegians reading this are probably shouting 'We are!' I realise all this is a poor excuse for not embracing a world-renowned book festival on my doorstep – almost.

I have attended events in the past such as Richard Ford and James Kelman. I even had the misfortune to sit through a turgid hour of Pat Kane, lead singer in the Scottish band, Hue and Cry, pontificate on his book *The Play Ethic*, which boasted of being 'a manifesto for a different way of living', but which turned out to be a lot of self-indulgent mumbo-jumbo trying to masquerade as an intellectual theory. So there is a vague feeling of guilt which gnaws at me throughout the fortnight, though not enough to make me jump in my car or buy a train ticket and head through to Edinburgh.

As I mentioned before, I'm a regular customer in my local Oxfam shop, and I've picked up a few good novels in recent months. Indeed, there are occasions as I'm scanning the shelves and recognise books I already own when the thought crosses my mind that, while I'm at work, Karen is surreptitiously removing books from my shelves and donating them to Oxfam. She denies this vehemently when I half-jokingly suggest it to her. I also wonder whether investing in charity shops, similar to using Amazon, is undermining the future of traditional books shops, accepting that there is no comparison, economic or moral, between Oxfam and Amazon.

I pick up Howard Jacobson's *The Finkler Question* at the charity shop. It's another Booker Prize-winning novel, having won the award in 2010, and as I start reading it, the germ of an idea begins the form. The shortlist for this year's prize is being announced on September 10, and I wonder if I could read all six of the books before the winner is revealed on

October 15. In the meantime, I read Jacobson's novel. It's not as funny as it's billed, but it's an interesting novel that looks at the issue of Jewish identity, and what it means to be a Jew in Britain today, particularly in relation to Zionism and the state of Israel. I'm in no position to judge whether *The Finkler Question* deserved to win the Booker Prize, certainly without reading the other books on the 2010 shortlist, but it is not anywhere near as good as J.M. Coetzee's *Disgrace* or Hilary Mantel's *Wolf Hall*.

The cover of *Ratlines* by Stuart Neville catches my eye in a book shop one day. Okay, I won't lie, it was Tesco, which is even more morally reprehensible, as a bibliophile and a writer, than choosing to shop online, but it's the author's introduction which really grabs my attention and makes me want to read the novel, which I do quickly and with much relish.

'This is fiction, not history. Although this novel is inspired by real people and locations, all of the events herein are entirely imagined.

These things are known to be true: Dozens of Nazis and Axis collaborators sought refuge in Ireland following the Second World War; in 1957, Otto Skorzeny was welcomed to a country club reception by the young politician Charles Haughey; Otto Skorzeny purchased Martinstown House in Kildare in 1959; in 1963, in response to a question by Dr Noel Browne TD, the Minister for Justice Charles Haughey told the Irish parliament that Otto Skorzeny had never been resident in Ireland.'

Now if that's not enough to make you all want to rush out and buy *Ratlines*, then I don't know what's wrong with you. Stuart Neville has written a brilliant thriller, and it would make a superb film, although no doubt with some mis-casting that would probably see Tom Cruise as the main German baddy, Otto Skorzeny, a German war hero who masterminded the rescue of Benito Mussolini in 1943. After the war, he was involved in the ODESSA network, which helped Nazi SS officers avoid capture and prosecution for war crimes. The lines of escape they set up were called 'ratlines'. It's the tiny fragments of truth in the author's introduction which intrigue me, while he doesn't disappoint with his writing. I'm also envious of Neville's ability to spot a story from such fragments and turn it into a full-blown novel. Maybe he was the only person to piece together a work of fiction from such rudimentary facts, or maybe he was just the quickest off the mark. Either way, the end result is impressive.

On August 20, it's announced that Elmore Leonard has died at the age of eighty-seven. The American writer is considered a master of crime novels, some of which were turned into films, while he also wrote a number of fine Western novels. I'd only recently read a book of his short stories at the end of June which reminded me what a great writer he was. He also left behind the set of writing rules I referred to before that should be a prerequisite for all aspiring and established novelists.

1. Never open a book with weather.

2. Avoid prologues.

3. Never use a verb other than 'said' to carry dialogue.

4. Never use an adverb to modify the verb 'said'…he admonished gravely.

5. Keep your exclamation points under control. You are allowed no more than two or three per 100,000 words of prose.

6. Never use the words 'suddenly' or 'all hell broke loose.'

7. Use regional dialect, patois, sparingly.

8. Avoid detailed descriptions of characters.

9. Don't go into great detail describing places and things.

10. Try to leave out the part that readers tend to skip.

My most important rule is one that sums up the 10… If it sounds like writing, I rewrite it.

This is an abbreviated version. You can check out the Internet for Leonard's complete advice, particularly if you want to write, and you won't go far wrong if you stick to his wise words, so long as you've got some writing talent too, I suppose. Last year, to celebrate these words of wisdom, *The Guardian* newspaper asked a number of writers to come up with their own list of rules or advice on writing. It inspired me to compile my own top ten tips for writing, which I first published in a blog on my website, and later used when I was speaking at events to promote my books.

1. Write.
2. Read.
3. Enjoy what you're writing.
4. Write about what you know (unless you don't know very much, or what you do know is boring, in which case write about anything you like).
5. Read what you've written aloud.
6. Don't get Sky+
7. Don't re-write until you've finished a first draft.
8. Live your life.
9. Don't moan about it.
10. Write.

The one which always gets the biggest laugh at any talk I give is Number Six. For me, Sky+ is one of the best inventions ever, and also one of the biggest potential enemies of a writer. With Sky+ there is now always something to watch on television which means that an even greater discipline in setting aside time to write is required, which isn't easy. And keep the Internet turned off as well while you're at it. Emails and Facebook and Twitter are horribly addictive and very distracting. Incidentally, I love Sky+.

My favourite piece of advice, in as much as anyone might actually listen to anything I have to say, is Number Eight. Richard Ford, whose work I absolutely love, offered, as one of his writing tips, the advice not to have children. I disagree. Absolutely. Children are not a distraction. It might just mean that you have to work harder at finding the time to write around family life, but you can do it. And when all's said and done, a book is just a book, but your children are the greatest blessing you will ever have. And if I only ever achieve one thing in life to be proud of, it would be in having children who have grown up to be adults whom I actually like. You can keep your Booker Prize.

In saying that, amongst my children, opinion is divided towards my books. Louise, who is the oldest, has now managed to read two of them, and plans to tackle the third at some point this year. Rebecca has read all three of the books, and did so as and when they were first published. Andrew hasn't read any of them, nor does he intend to. When *Saints and Sinners* was published back in 2010, I gave all three of them a copy with a personal message written inside. A couple of weeks later, Andrew came into the living room and declared: 'Dad, I'm not going to read your book. Books aren't for me. I'm just going to wait until the film comes out.' Are you reading this, Hollywood? Someone call me and make this happen, if not for me, then for my son. He deserves to know what happens in these books.

Having returned to the joy of physical books on my return from holiday, I loaned my Kindle to a work colleague who, somewhat embarrassed, admits to me one day that it has been stolen during a break-in at his flat. I am not unduly upset. It wasn't his fault, after all, and it could even lead to the best-read burglar in Glasgow. While he offers to buy a replacement, I'm actually able to use Rebecca's old Kindle – she's graduated to a Kindle Fire HD – and once I re-register it in my name, my Kindle library magically appears on my new device. Sometimes the wonder of modern technology is just that – wonderful.

I've always had it in my head that George Orwell's *1984* and Aldous Huxley's *Brave New World* were inadvertent companions in offering bleak but eerily prophetic visions of the future. I've read *1984* on several occasions but I hadn't tackled *Brave New World* before now, so I decide to make amends. What's important to remember about both novels is when they were published. Orwell's novel came out in 1948, while Huxley's was published, remarkably, in 1932. Both of them have a perception about the future that is uncanny. Huxley's *Brave New World* tackles issues of eugenics, social engineering and the reverence of science as a way of living and controlling lives, as well as being a substitute for God and religion. It's a fascinating book, which also raises sociological questions of nature versus nurture.

It continues to resonate, particularly in our vacuous twenty-first century world with its desire for instant and meaningless gratification, and the homogeneity of our culture within a society that has stopped valuing individuals and individuality. I discover, too, from the Internet that Orwell and Huxley disagreed about the book. Apparently, Orwell believed that *Brave New World* took its inspiration from a 1920s dystopian novel entitled *We* by Yevgeny Zamyatin. Huxley dismissed the idea, claiming he wrote his book before he'd ever heard of *We*, but Orwell always believed his fellow author was lying. By the time I've finished *Brave New World*, my mind is set on tackling my Booker Prize challenge. I am going to try and read all six books in thirty-five days, from September 10 to October 15.

It's also announced, on August 30, that the Irish poet, Seamus Heaney has died at the age of seventy-four. I feel that this book, as well as recording my reading habits, is also becoming a chronicle of literary figures who have written their final chapter in 2013. I can't say that I'm particularly knowledgeable or proficient when it comes to poetry. You've already seen some of my efforts, so you know it's not false modesty on my part. I have a handful of poetry books hidden away on my shelves, but I rarely ever dip into them. Still, I do watch a couple of documentary tributes to Heaney, regarded as one of Ireland's finest ever poets. What does strike me is how much more captivating poetry is when it is read aloud, particularly in a voice as rich and melodic as Heaney's. I decide to buy an anthology of Heaney's poetry on the strength of these programmes, and it takes up temporary residence at the side of my bed.

In the build-up to the Booker Prize shortlist being announced, I start reading *Doctor Zhivago* by Boris Pasternak. I quickly get bogged down, and after about ninety pages I'm losing the will to live. For some reason, I have a mental block with Russian novels. I think it might have something to do with the countless derivations of a person's name which are used in each book, giving the impression that there's a cast of thousands when there might only be a handful of characters. I had the same problems with Dostoevsky's *Crime and Punishment*, and I'm in turmoil for a couple of days over whether to persevere with Pasternak's book. In the end, I give up and put it back on the shelf. It may well remain there for the rest of its, and my life. It's probably not the right thing to do, although I refer you back to the account of my experiences with Salman Rushdie. Indeed, the bold Mr. Rushdie once said:

'A book is a version of the world. If you do not like it, ignore it; or offer your own version in return.'

It is these words that I use to justify my action. *Doctor Zhivago* is only the second book that I've given up on this year, after *A Fan's Notes* by Frederick Exley, while there have been a few, in particular a couple of Roddy Doyle's novels, which I persevered with, even though I wasn't enjoying the experience. So Pasternak's 'classic' of Russian literature has failed me, or I have failed it. Maybe it wasn't meant to be. I'll just watch the film instead.

Having 'escaped' from early twentieth-century Russia, I start reading *The Imperfectionists* by Tom Rachman, which turns out to be a great decision, because it is an absolute gem of a book. Set in an English language newspaper based in Rome, the novel tells the various and varied stories of the characters who staff the paper in individual yet interlinked chapters. Each chapter is a brilliantly crafted short story in its own right, populated with a cast of fascinating or horrifying characters, some of whom I recognise from my own journalistic career. Rachman's novel, apart from being a superb character study, is also a great chronicle of the changing face of the newspaper industry.

Having been involved in journalism for over twenty years, I obviously have a vested interest in the future of newspapers. Like books, and indeed, all printed material, they face an unprecedented challenge from electronic/digital platforms, along with an increasing apathy towards reading itself. Many people have got out of the habit of reading, whether through disinterest or through a misguided and mistaken belief that they 'don't have the time'. The author, JK Rowling, counters this misnomer perfectly when she says:

'I never need to find time to read. When people say to me, 'Oh, yeah, I love reading. I would love to read, but I just don't have time,' I'm thinking, 'How can you not have time? I read when I'm drying my hair. I read in the bath. I read when I'm sitting in the bathroom. Pretty much anywhere I can do the job one-handed, I read.'

I'm obviously encouraged by JK Rowling's words, though they shouldn't come as a surprise. It's hard to imagine her having the success she has enjoyed as a writer if she wasn't also a reader. Sadly, I have to confess that part of me is also delighted at Ms Rowling's declaration that she reads in the bathroom ... for perfectly innocent reasons, I hasten to add.

I like to read in the bathroom, in much the same way as many people do, although I've always believed it to be a predominantly male habit. I have never made any apologies for this, despite the dismay, disgust and disdain which has always greeted my departure for the bathroom with a book or newspaper ensconced under my arm. My own dismay comes from Karen's refusal to install a bookcase in the bathroom, despite repeated requests. JK Rowling may well be amongst a minority of women who have this habit, but she's a welcome and renowned addition to the Cludgie Reading Club.

I finish reading *The Imperfectionists*, not in the bathroom but in bed, and with perfect timing. It's September 9 and in just under twelve hours' time, at half past ten on Wednesday, September 10, the shortlist for this year's Booker Prize will be announced. Six books – and authors – will take a step closer to scooping the prestigious award, and my intention is to read them all before the winner is announced on October 15. I've already got a plan for tomorrow. I will head to Waterstone's in Sauchiehall Street, Glasgow, after work and buy all six books so that I can start my challenge right away. I know I can't afford to lose a single day if I want to read them all within my self-imposed deadline.

Don't Judge A Booker By Its Cover

'I only read factual books. I can't think of ... I mean, novels are just a waste of fucking time. I can't suspend belief in reality ... I just end up thinking, 'This isn't fucking true.' I like reading about things that have actually happened.'

Noel Gallagher

At half past ten on the morning of Tuesday, September 10, the shortlist for the 2013 Man Booker Prize – to give it its full title – is announced, with six novels selected. The prize is twofold; there is the kudos that comes with winning such a prestigious award, which is an affirmation for a writer of their ability, while there is a natural boost in sales which increase every step of the way – from longlist to shortlist, and then to winner. And, of course, there is the small matter of a £50,000 first prize.

The Booker Prize, which is described as 'a literary prize awarded each year for the best original full-length novel, written in the English language, by a citizen of the Commonwealth of Nations, the Republic of Ireland, or Zimbabwe', has been in existence since 1969 when P.H. Newby won it for his novel, *Something To Answer For.* He picked up a cheque for £5,000. To date, there have been forty-five winners, of which I have only read seven – which includes three this year. I've also read a further five novels that were short-listed. Given that there have been two hundred and sixty-one books nominated for the Prize since 1969, that's not a good success rate. In fact, that's just 4.6% of the books which have made it as far as the shortlist since the prize began. Considering the fact that I would one day like to win the Booker Prize – okay, stop that laughing – I should really know more about all the novels that have come before my, as yet unwritten, prize-winning tome.

For the record, the prize-winners I've read are: *Schindler's Ark* by Thomas Keneally (1982), *Sacred Hunger* by Barry Unsworth (1992), *Paddy Clarke Ha Ha Ha* by Roddy Doyle (1993), *Disgrace* by JM Coetzee (1999), *The Life of Pi* by Yann Martel (2002), *Wolf Hall* by Hilary Mantel (2009) and *The Finkler Question* by Howard Jacobson (2010).

The shortlisted books are: *Confederates* by Thomas Keneally (1979), *The Van* by Roddy Doyle (1991), *The Butcher Boy* by Patrick McCabe (1992), *Our Fathers* by Andrew O'Hagan (1999) and *The Dark Room* by Rachel Seiffert (2001).

For goodness sake, I haven't even read *How Late It Was, How Late* by James Kelman, which won the prize in 1994, and as a Glaswegian that's a poor admission. Kelman's novel attracted an unprecedented level of controversy when it won the prize due to the fact it's written in the vernacular of Glasgow and includes a liberal smattering of the word 'fuck', amongst other profanities. One of the judges, Rabbi Julia Neuberger, threatened to resign if it won, and upon the book being granted the prize, stormed off the panel, saying, 'Frankly, it's crap.' Kelman's response, in his acceptance speech, addressed the 'controversy', saying:

'One of the remaining freedoms we have as writers is the blank page. Let no one prescribe how we should fill it whether by good or bad intention, not the media, not the publisher, not the book trade; not anyone. In spite of everything it is the creation of art that keeps us going.'

Having successfully completed a Kelman novel this year, and enjoyed it too, *How Late It Was, How Late* is now on my radar, but not over the next thirty-five days. By 6pm on September 10, I am at Waterstone's looking to buy all six of the shortlisted books. It's here that I encounter my first problem. No-one in the shop appears to know that the shortlist has been announced. Now maybe it's naïve of me to have expected the books to be prominently displayed, but surely Glasgow's biggest book shop would at least have been aware of the latest news about this important literary prize?

It's not that it was difficult to find out. I don't know how the very first shortlist was announced back in 1969, but in 2013 the wonderful world of Twitter breaks the news, using a quirky video that has the longlisted novels lined up on a book shelf and a number of them are removed until only the six shortlisted ones remain.

Evidently, no-one at Waterstone's was monitoring social media during the day which, on the one hand, is commendable, since it means they've all been hard at work, but since selling books is their raison d'être, and people buy books that are shortlisted for major literary prizes, it seems like a dreadful oversight. Armed with a printed list of the novels, I check to make sure all of the books are in stock and then approach a member of staff.

'Excuse me, I'm looking to buy the Booker Prize shortlisted books?'

'Is that the list there?' she says, nodding towards the sheet of paper in my hand.

'Yes.'

'Have they announced it then?'

'Yes, it was this morning.'

'Oh, I didn't realise. Can I see your list?'

I hand the sheet of paper over to her.

'Would you offer a discount if I bought all six books?' I ask.

'No,' she replies, still scanning the piece of paper.

'Nothing at all?'

'No.'

'Not even if I bought all six?'

'Sorry, we're not allowed. It's only head office which can make that decision.'

The Waterstone's girl is apologetic, but it seems to crystallise one of the major problems with book shops and why they are slowly disappearing from our high streets. Not only do they not know the composition of the shortlist of Britain's most prestigious literary prize, but they aren't offering any incentives for people wanting to read the books.

In the end, I buy three of the books from Waterstone's and later order another two via Amazon. I decide to pick up the sixth book later. With just thirty-five days until the winner is announced, I dive straight into the first book – *We Need New Names* by NoViolet Bulawayo.

The author is from Zimbabwe, though she now lives in the United States, and I suspect there is a biographical element to the novel. NoViolet Bulawayo has evidently adopted one of the classic pieces of advice given to would-be writers – write what you know. Her novel is set mainly in Zimbabwe and tells the story of the ongoing tragedy in that country, a human catastrophe largely ignored by the world because Zimbabwe has nothing to offer in terms of coveted natural resources. The novel has a brilliant narrator, Darling, who lives in a shanty town, ironically called Paradise, though she still remembers a time when she and her family lived in a proper house. There is a theme of things falling apart, in her life and in her country, a reference, indirect or otherwise, to Chinua Achebe's classic African novel, *Things Fall Apart*. Darling manages to leave her country, moving to the United States, though her new life doesn't necessarily bring her the happiness she thought it would when she was living in Zimbabwe. Darling's voice remains a memorable one long after I've finished the book, which I do within a couple of days. I've got off to a good start.

This year's Booker Prize shortlist boasts a number of firsts; NoViolet Bulawayo is the first black African woman and first Zimbabwean writer to be shortlisted, while Colm Toibin's novel, *The Testament of Mary,* is the 'shortest' book ever selected, at just one hundred and one pages. Eleanor Catton, meanwhile, is the youngest novelist to have reached this stage, at just twenty-seven, while her novel, *The Luminaries,* is the 'longest' book ever selected, weighing in at a mammoth eight hundred and thirty-two pages. I decide to tackle it next, figuring that because of its length, it's going to take me longer to read and it's better to start now rather than leave it until last when I might end up running out of time.

As a physical product, *The Luminaries* is absolutely beautiful. It looks like a Bible, complete with gold page marker, and anyone who has opted to buy the electronic version is missing out on a wonderful literary experience. Any debate on physical versus e-books is a foregone conclusion when you hold this book in your hand. There is a thrill every time I pick it up and I have an urge to read it out loud like I'm reading at Mass on a Sunday. I resist that urge, I hasten to add. It's bad enough that the bedside lamp remains on while Karen tries to get to sleep. I dread to imagine her reaction should I start reading out loud.

In the midst of reading *The Luminaries*, the Booker Prize hits the headlines when it's announced that, from 2014, the award will consider authors from anywhere in the world, so long as their work in written in English and published in the United Kingdom. It means, in effect, that the Americans are coming. The news immediately sparks controversy in literary circles. The aim, clearly, is to raise the global profile of the award and open it up to more authors. The fear, just as clearly, is that it could lose its distinctiveness and lead to a downgrading of British writers. If I have to take sides in this argument, I would have to agree with those who think it's a bad idea, though there are selfish reasons for that. Expanding the award means that it will make it even more difficult for me to win it, though admittedly my main stumbling block is that I haven't actually written anything worthy of being nominated in the first place.

I am progressing steadily with *The Luminaries* and, as well as being a stunning book to look at, it's also an extraordinary feat of storytelling. To write a novel of eight hundred and thirty-two pages and remain in control of the narrative and characters from first page until last is a real and rare talent, and a cocktail of admiration, jealousy and depression swirls about my mind. Eleanor Catton is only twenty-seven, for goodness sake, twenty years younger than me. Her novel is set during the gold rush in New Zealand in the 1860s, and is a tale of murder, mystery and intrigue that never wilts. I have to confess that there are some elements of the novel which critics have referred to and praised which have passed me by.

The Guardian describes how the book is organised '... according to astrological principles, so that characters are not only associated with signs of the zodiac, or the sun and moon (the 'luminaries' of the title), but interact with each other according to the predetermined movement of the heavens, while each of the novel's twelve parts decreases in length over the course of the book to mimic the moon waning through its lunar cycle.'

Not knowing or realising that doesn't lessen my enjoyment of the book and there is a real sense of achievement in finishing it. It's certainly one of the longest novels I've ever read. If there is a disappointment, and it's just a slight one, it is in the ending which jumps from the present to the past to bring the tale to a conclusion, and it feels, to me, as if it slightly drifts when perhaps I was hoping for a dramatic finale.

Not surprisingly, it takes me much longer than a couple of days to read *The Luminaries*, but having done so I move quickly on to *Harvest* by Jim Crace. Set in an unnamed village at an unspecified period of the past, the novel describes how a settled way of life is completely overturned and destroyed in the space of just seven days. A group of strangers arrive and are blamed for something they didn't do. They are subsequently punished which, though seemingly innocuous at first, appears to herald a series of increasingly disastrous events for the village. At the same time, the village is taken over by another owner who has different ideas of what the land is to be used for, which has an even more devastating impact on the inhabitants. *Harvest* tackles themes of change, xenophobia and how an apparent 'paradise' on earth can be quickly destroyed by man's inhumanity to man.

Crace's novel, which he claims will be his last ever work of fiction – so at least that's one less rival for a future Booker award – is apparently being mentioned by many critics and bookmakers as the favourite to win this year's prize. I'm guessing that more critics than bookmakers will be talking about this, since I can't imagine walking into any bookies in Glasgow and placing a bet on the Booker Prize. I'd probably be laughed – or kicked – out of the shop. I'm also guessing that, if Waterstone's didn't even know the shortlist had been announced, Ladbrokes *et al* will be completely oblivious to the Booker's existence. *Harvest* is a fine novel, and it's easy to spot the quality of the writing, but out of the three books I've read so far, it's actually in third place for me.

I'm halfway towards my target and pleased with how it's going so far. With three books to go, including Toibin's one-hundred-and-one-page novel, I'm confident that I'll complete the list by October 15. Next up is *The Lowland* by Jhumpa Lahiri, a family saga which veers between interest and irritation. The characters provoke the same reaction in me as was the case when I read John Williams' *Stoner*. There are times when I just want to step in and give them a shake and tell them to take charge of what is happening in their lives rather than letting it be dictated by others, including the author. Maybe that's what real life is actually like – a frustrating existence of thwarted dreams and ambitions. What a dreadful thought.

The novel tells the story of two brothers in India and what happens when something catastrophic happens in their lives. It examines family relationships, which shift and change shape throughout the course of a life. Overall, it's still an eminently readable and enjoyable novel though I know even as I'm reading it that it won't be my favourite out of the six. If it's any consolation to Jhumpa Lahiri, and I'm sure she doesn't care what my opinion is, then she wins hands-down for the best author picture on the inside cover of her book. Actually, I'm sure if she reads this, she's liable to be furious rather than flattered, but as a friend of mine often says, 'I'm only saying what everyone else is thinking.'

This year's prize-giving ceremony is being held at London's Guildhall, and the prize is being presented by the Duchess of Cornwall, Camilla Parker-Bowles, who is Prince

Charles' missus. It seems to be a regular pastime/occupation for the spouses of political leaders or prominent people for them to have some sort of connection to literacy. Laura Bush, wife of former American president, George W. Bush, immediately springs to mind. I think everyone suspected she was the one with brains in that White House, and given that she began her career as a teacher and then librarian, it would probably be somewhat unkind to suggest the subject of literacy was given to her merely as something to occupy her time. It seems, and I'm happy to accept it as true, that she has a genuine interest in the subject, and she was involved in many literacy projects both before and during her husband's presidency. In 2006, she was also made honorary ambassador for the United Nations' Decade of Literacy, while the Laura Bush Foundation for America's Libraries gives out over one million dollars every year in grants to American schools. So we'll give Laura the benefit of the doubt.

I don't know too much about Camilla, though a cursory Google search does reveal that she is a big supporter of literacy too and, in particular, child literacy projects. Her husband talks to plants, apparently. I don't think the two things are related, but I thought I'd mention it anyway.

I've managed to read four of the books by October 6, giving me nine days to finish the last two on the shortlist. Ruth Oseki's book is the only one I haven't already bought, and when I go in to Waterstone's to buy it, a member of staff who sells me the book tells me she really enjoyed it. It's always nice to get such a recommendation, and I start the book with a burst of enthusiasm that owes as much to the fact that I can see the finishing line and with it a sense of achievement. *A Tale For The Time Being* is an unusual and beguiling novel, which tells two stories – that of a teenage Japanese girl, Nau, who has returned to Japan after her dad lost his job in the United States, and that of the novelist herself, who accidentally discovers Nau's story through a diary washed up on a beach at some point after the devastating tsunami which struck Japan in 2011. The book examines the relationship between a novelist, their subject and the reader, which is not as confusing as it sounds, though the explanation of quantum mechanics at the end certainly is. There are a number of Appendixes at the end of the novel. I would recommend skim-reading them. That's not general advice for appendixes. There are three at the end of this book, all of them fascinating and well worth reading.

Finishing the book, I realise the task for the Booker judging panel has been a tough one – in the first instance to choose a longlist, and then a shortlist, and now from that, a winner. Ruth Oseki's book is an interesting and clever one, but it, too, doesn't manage to push its way to the top of my chart, which remains, for now, a battle between *We Need New Names* and *The Luminaries*.

And so to the last of the shortlisted books. It's also the shortest book and it takes no time at all to finish it. Colm Toibin's *The Testament of Mary* tells the story of Mary, the mother of Jesus, as she lives with the grief of her son's death. Reflecting on the events leading up his crucifixion, Mary's testament offers a new and intriguing perspective on a story that is already so familiar, including the miracles that the Bible attributes to her son. Mary is visited regularly by two of Jesus' disciples, who talk to her about her son's life, over and over again, hoping to shape her words and memories to suit the story they are forging of the events they were witness to.

I finish the book on October 13, two days ahead of the winner being announced. I have to admit that I'm quite pleased with myself, having read six books in thirty-three days, and six books of perceived quality. I've enjoyed them all, to varying degrees, and it means that I can watch a *BBC Review* programme on the Booker Prize shortlist and know about all the books they're discussing, even if I still don't understand much of what the panel of 'experts' are saying. These programmes can be pretentious, although I find myself harbouring a desire to be a guest on them so that I, too, can pontificate on the merits of whatever books are being featured.

So, having read all six books the winner, for me, has to be Colm Toibin's novel, *The Testament of Mary*. It is a short book, but the story is beautifully and poetically told, and as someone who has always found devotion to Our Lady a comforting one, particularly through the Rosary, it is enlightening to hear an imagining of her voice for the first time, one of the many female voices not really heard in the Gospels.

I, therefore, take more than a passing interest in the awards ceremony, which is screened live on the *BBC News 24* channel. And the actual winner is ... Eleanor Catton's novel, *The Luminaries*. I have to admit to a touch of disappointment at the news, if only because the judges' choice doesn't concur with mine, though I can't begrudge Catton her moment of glory, not least because her novel truly is a celebration of everything that is beautiful about a physical book. At the age of twenty-eight – she celebrated her birthday towards the end of September – she is the youngest ever Booker winner, and with only her second novel. I suspect there will be more great novels from her to come, though winning this prize will undoubtedly put pressure on her for her next work.

In the short-term, however, there is the fame – the announcement is reported throughout the world; the fortune – she has walked away with a cheque for £50,000; and there is the inevitable increase in book sales, which can be seen from the table of previous winners below.

Year	Author/Title	Week before	Prize week	Change
2003	DBC Pierre: Vernon God Little	509	8,627	1,595%
2004	Alan Hollinghurst: The Line of Beauty	422	4,390	940%
2005	John Banville: The Sea	601	6,327	953%
2006	Kiran Desai: The Inheritance of Loss	534	4,726	785%
2007	Anne Enright: The Gathering	434	6,001	1,283%
2008	Aravind Adiga: The White Tiger	463	8,033	1,653%
2009	Hilary Mantel: Wolf Hall	3,146	17,703	463%
2010	Howard Jacobson: The Finkler Question	627	12,650	1,918%
2011	Julian Barnes: The Sense of an Ending	2,535	14,534	473%
2012	Hilary Mantel: Bring Up The Bodies	1,846	10,605	474%

Source: Nielsen Bookscan

Meanwhile, having survived, and actually enjoyed my

Booker Prize experience, I take some time scanning the bookshelves for something different after so much quality literature. In the end, I opt for something that has a religious theme to it, in keeping with the last of the shortlisted books I read.

There's More To Life Than Books, But Not Much More

'You know you've read a good book when you turn the last page and feel a little as if you've lost a friend.'

Paul Sweeney

Michel Faber's novel, *The Fire Gospel,* is a short book which tells the story of a fifth gospel discovered in a bombed-out museum in Iraq by an American academic. He translates it from the ancient Aramaic language and gets it published, sparking great controversy as it provides an eye-witness account of Jesus' life, as opposed to the four retrospective gospels of Matthew, Mark, Luke and John. The gospel according to Malchus, not surprisingly, sells millions of copies, but it doesn't bring its author, Theo Griepenkerl, happiness even as it brings him wealth. The novel is a satire on religion, with a side-swipe at the world of publishing too. I found it interesting to read on the back of Colm Toibin's *The Testament of Mary*, which offers another perspective on what has long been a familiar story. Has the last two thousand years, and the beliefs of countless billions, relied on the words of four men which may be fact or fiction, or a confusing mixture of both?

I don't think either novel has undermined my faith, faltering though it often is, but it certainly makes me think about it in relation to organised religion, in my case the Catholic Church. My attitude and relationship with the Church is ambivalent at the best of times. I can't put to one side the 'sins of the fathers', and every new documentary that offers fresh revelations on the terrible misdeeds of the Church, particularly in relation to the abuse of children and subsequent hierarchical cover-ups, leaves me angry and sad, given that I grew up in a devout Catholic family where the Church was part and parcel of our lives. Yet, whenever I find myself inside a church now – for a baptism, wedding or funeral – I still have feelings of being 'home', the pull of the faith always there.

The Fire Gospel is entertaining enough but it's nowhere near as good as Faber's masterpiece, *The Crimson Petal and the White.* If you haven't read that book, then I suggest you make amends. It is a majestic work of fiction.

Footballers don't have a reputation for being amongst society's great intellectuals, and it's not surprising to discover that reading ranks pretty low on their list of pastimes or abilities, even though many of them manage to 'write' best-selling autobiographies, the majority of which are asinine. Indeed, I would go as far to say that, given a choice, I'd still attempt to read *The Satanic Verses* before most football autobiographies. There are honourable exceptions such as Tony Cascarino and Paul McGrath, or even the current Celtic manager, Neil Lennon, who courageously discussed his battle with depression in his book, but by and large they have as much value as Pippa Middleton's book of party tips.

So I'm more than a little surprised when the current England manager, Roy Hodgson, in a post-match interview after seeing his side qualify for the 2014 World Cup tournament, reveals that he'll be going home to continue reading *Stoner* by John Williams. Maybe Hodgson, like me, was convinced by the social media publicity blitz, though at the age of sixty-six, he doesn't strike me as the sort of person who uses Facebook or Twitter. He does, however, appear to be an erudite and intelligent man, which puts him at odds with the majority of the English press who follow the national team. I wonder how many journalists started writing sensational stories about Hodgson's drugs-related reading material before wiser heads at their newspapers prevailed.

The Unlikely Pilgrimage of Harold Fry by Rachel Joyce is next up for me, and it comes with a plethora of positive recommendations plastered across the cover. 'Impossible to put down,' according to *The Times*, 'Touching and charming,' says the *Sunday Express*, 'One of the best books you'll read this year,' declares the *Daily Mail*, while the *Sunday Times* states that the book is 'At times almost unbearably moving.' With such abundant praise, how could I possibly not love this book? It is actually quite good, although it's hardly surprising that it doesn't live up to its billing.

The premise is an interesting one – Harold Fry leaves his home one morning to post a letter to an old friend, and then decides to start walking from one end of England to the other to see that person because she is dying. He believes that, by undertaking this daunting pilgrimage, he can save her. It reminds me very much of *Forrest Gump*, and like the film, it becomes a bit too sickly sweet by the end. The publishers can put that comment on the cover of future editions if they want to. I won't mind.

For those of you who have stayed with me on this literary journey, you may remember that I have mentioned on occasion that I like to play the acoustic guitar, usually at family parties in the early hours of the morning when everyone is drunk and my limitations go unnoticed. I've been playing the guitar since I've been about thirty. I actually got my first guitar as a twenty-first birthday present from my sisters, but apart from a few half-hearted attempts to learn to play it – which lasted until I knocked the instrument out of tune – it gathered dust in a cupboard. Then I heard the Oasis song, *Wonderwall*, and I knew I had to learn to play it. It was my inspiration to dust down the acoustic guitar, get it restrung and tuned, invest in an electronic tuner – which turned out to be a God-send – and practise in earnest. *Wonderwall* wasn't the first song I learned, but it remains one of my favourites, and I felt a real sense of achievement when I did finally learn to play it; I was going to say 'master it', but anyone who has heard me play the song will know that it's definitely not been mastered.

I should, therefore, react with more dismay when Noel Gallagher, the man who wrote *Wonderwall*, declares in an interview with *GQ* magazine that '...novels are just a waste of fucking time...' You may already recognise the quote, since I used it at the beginning of Chapter Nine. I suspect, however, that Gallagher's just being a bit of rascal. The interview goes like this:

Isn't your wife religious?
She has been known to attend church.
That's one of the first signs.
I've never seen her do it. But you know when you see these people standing on soapboxes banging on about religion or politics, or worse - when they're combining the fucking two? Really? If you're thinking that anything written in a book 2,000 years old bears any relevance to anything these days...
What would be our Bible, then?
I only read factual books. I can't think of... I mean, novels are just a waste of fucking time. I can't suspend belief in reality... I just end up thinking, 'This isn't fucking true.' I like reading about things that have actually happened. I'm reading this book at the minute - The Kennedy Tapes. It's all about the Cold War, the Cuban Missile Crisis - I can get into that. Thinking, 'Wow, this actually fucking happened, they came that close to blowing the world up!' But... what fucking winds me up about books...
This is already the best sentence I've ever heard.
...is, like... my missus will come in with a book and it will be titled - and there's a lot of these, you can substitute any word, it's like a Rubik's Cube of shit titles - it'll be entitled The Incontinence Of Elephants. And I'll say 'What's that book about?' And she'll say, 'Oh it's about a girl and this load of fucking nutters...' Right... so it's not about elephants, then? Why the fuck is it called The Incontinence Of Elephants? Another one: The Tales Of The Clumsy Beekeeper. What's that about? 'Oh it's about the French Revolution.' Right, fuck off. If you're writing a book about a child who's locked in a fucking cupboard during the fucking Second World War... he's never seen an elephant. Never mind a fucking giraffe.'

The comments, not surprisingly, generate plenty of

controversy and publicity, and I suspect that's the whole point of them, if not from Gallagher's perspective, then certainly from the magazine's point of view, since it publicises the issue they want to sell. I may be doing Noel Gallagher a disservice and he's actually wanting to start a proper debate on the merits, or not, of fiction, but I doubt it. To be fair to the talented brother from Oasis, he does at least still read non-fiction books, unlike American singer Kanye West, who proudly declares: 'I would never want a book's autograph. I am a proud non-reader of books.' I've never met the bold Kanye, and I can't envisage a scenario when we'd ever be in the same room, but his disparaging attitude towards books is not an admirable one.

It reminds me of the time that I read an interview with Fran Healy, lead singer of the band, Travis, when he declared with evident pride that he didn't read books. I was a big fan of the band at the time, though that admiration quickly dissipated after that point. However, it is the words of American film director, John Waters, which I hope would perhaps counsel Kanye West, Fran Healy and those of their ilk about the potential consequences of being too dismissive of books, and offer a warning to future generations who would adopt the same attitude. There could be unpredictable consequences. Waters' dating advice is thus:

'We need to make books cool again. If you go home with somebody and they don't have books, don't fuck them. Don't sleep with people who don't read!'

The eagle-eyed amongst you will have noticed that I have used the full quote here, whereas, for reasons of taste and sensitivity, I opted to omit the profanity from the back cover.

I was going to write that music plays an important part in my life, but that's just a cliché and it's not even true. It's not important, certainly not since I got married and had children, in much the same way that sport can't be the central focus of your life when you become a parent. However, music is something that I do enjoy. I listen to music when I'm writing, and the type of music varies, depending on what I'm working on. For example, right now as I'm writing these words I'm listening to Rodriquez and the *Searching for Sugar Man* film soundtrack. The songs are brilliant, while the film is one of the best documentaries I've ever seen. When I was writing my 'Costello trilogy', I listened to a lot of Clannad; the books are set between Ireland, Scotland and America in the late nineteenth and early twentieth century, so it seemed appropriate. At other times, I've listened to Corinne Bailey Rae, some classic Simple Minds from the 1980s, and even Gregorian chant music.

A documentary on the demise of record shops also offers parallels and warnings to book shops. *Last Shop Standing* on Sky Arts 1 reflects on the heyday of record shops in the 1960s, '70s' and '80s, and explores their sad decline in the modern age. I'm not sure if there was ever a similar heyday for book shops, but as I've mentioned before, the changing buying habits of readers, along with technological innovations, are making it increasingly difficult for book shops to survive in the 'High Street'. Big names have already disappeared, such as Borders and Ottakars, while there are fewer and fewer Waterstone's outlets in town and city centres. I can be sanctimonious and self-righteous and declare that the future depends on the survival of independent book stores, but I'm part of the problem as much as I, like every reader, am also part of the solution. I need to start putting my money where my mouth is when it comes to buying my books.

My next book relates perfectly to the music theme of this chapter as it's Morrissey's autobiography called, simply, *Morrissey: The Autobiography*. The Smiths are one of my favourite bands while their music, in particular *What Difference Does It Make*, reminds me of being a teenager and going to Level Eight at Strathclyde University every weekend. That's where Karen and I met, back in the heady days of 1989, though it was actually at a Bad Manners concert. Neither of us were fans of the band, incidentally. They just happened to be playing there the night we drunkenly bumped into each other. The rest, as they say, is history... So I'm keen to read Morrissey's words. I give Rebecca money to get the book – fifteen pounds, since I don't know the price. It turns out to be £8.99. I get the book back, without any change. No surprise there, and I wouldn't mind so much but just a few weeks later it goes on sale in Tesco for just under four pounds. So if you're reading this, Rebecca, and I know that, unlike your siblings, you will be, you still owe me six pounds and one pence.

There is controversy even before Morrissey's book is released when it's announced that it is to be published on the Penguin Classics imprint. There is a debate over what makes 'a classic', and the merits of declaring a newly-published book as such. Critics line up to denounce the decision, saying it devalues the imprint and the genuine 'classics' on its list, while supporters, mainly fans of Morrissey and The Smiths, dismiss the criticism as literary snobbery. It seems pretty obvious to me that Penguin have made the decision purely as part of a marketing strategy, which guarantees lots of free publicity for the book and ensures that, whether or not it's an instant classic, it is an instant best-seller.

I want to love Morrissey's book, but there are a number of reasons why I don't. For one thing, I'm not a big fan of autobiographies in general. I find that they are, by their nature, self-indulgent, self-absorbed and self-serving. It's only to be expected, I suppose, but it makes them unappealing. By far the best autobiography I've ever read is Arthur Miller's *Timebends*, which is an engrossing tome by a gifted writer, although I should declare that Miller has always been one of my heroes, not least because he wrote *Death of a Salesman* AND he married Marilyn Monroe. Some of Morrissey's autobiography is interesting, particularly up to and including The Smiths' years, but the longer I stay with it, particularly in the post-Smiths era, the harder it is to read or enjoy. Morrissey appears to view himself as some sort of messianic figure, with followers rather than fans who hold sick people up for their saviour to provide a healing touch. And the long section about the acrimonious court case involving former members of The Smiths is turgid. Like most autobiographies, the author takes the credit for everything positive, and plays the victim for anything negative.

If you're a fan of The Smiths, you've probably already bought the book and read it, and if you have, I hope you enjoyed the experience more than I did; I still prefer to listen to the music. If you've not bought the book yet, but still want to read it, there's only one piece of advice I'll offer. Don't give my daughter money to get it for you. Go to Tesco and buy it yourself.

Based On A True Story

*'One of the great things about books is sometimes
there are some fantastic pictures.'*

George W. Bush

It seems like, over the past few years, journalists and bankers
have been vying to see who can claim the title of 'World's
Most Hated Profession'. I would add 'politician' to that
shortlist, and while, as a journalist, I would naturally opt for
one of the other categories, I can also understand why many
people have a disdain for the fourth estate. The fall-out from
the phone-hacking scandal involving the now defunct *News of
the World*, which led to the Leveson Inquiry into the culture,
practices and ethics of the British press, exposed the
nefarious activities of some journalists and newspapers, and
my reading matter seems appropriate, given that we're in the
middle of the phone-hacking trial involving a number of
former senior News International figures.

The aptly-titled *Muckraker* tells the story of W.T. Stead,
billed on the front cover of the book as 'Britain's first
investigative reporter'. I've borrowed the book from a
colleague along with a recommendation that I'll enjoy it. He's
not wrong. It's a fascinating story of a man who pioneered
what would now be acknowledged as tabloid journalism in
the straight-laced, superficially puritanical Victorian era of the
late nineteenth and early twentieth century. Stead's
extraordinary life saw him investigate child prostitution,
expose the secret love lives of the rich and famous, and make
countless powerful enemies along the way. He was, for a
short period of time, an influential figure in British political
circles, but he was never going to enjoy any longevity in that
position.

Stead became an increasingly eccentric character,

developing an obsession with the occult which pushed him to the periphery of society as a figure of ridicule, although he continued to chase the next big story. It led to his death, an extraordinary tale in itself but I won't spoil the book by revealing it here. Apart from the absence of telephones in Stead's era, and hence no phone-hacking, *Muckraker* has uncanny and unnerving parallels with the activities of the twenty-first century press. Lessons have evidently never been learned, or they've been long forgotten, and it would do many journalists no harm to read W. Sydney Robinson's biography of a fascinating character from journalism's annals, even if only as a salutary lesson on the negative impact of tabloid reporting that was as true in nineteenth century Britain as it is today.

Having read mainly fiction books throughout the year, I now tackle my second non-fiction book in a row. *Philomena* by Martin Sixsmith tells the story of an Irish woman's search for the son she had to give up in the 1950s. It is a heartbreaking tale, and one that does not paint the Catholic Church in a good light, like many revelations to have come out of Ireland over the past few years. Philomena Lee falls pregnant at the age of eighteen and is put into a convent by her family. She has to stay there for three years, working in one of the notorious laundries to gain her freedom, unless she somehow miraculously manages to find one hundred pounds to buy her way out. In the interim, the nuns who run the convent sell her son to an American family.

There are elements of the story which have harrowing parallels with Peter Mullan's stunning film, *The Magdalene Sisters*, and my brief description of the book, shocking though that might read, does not even begin to tell the full story of Philomena and the search for her son. That story has been turned into a film starring Judi Dench and Steve Coogan and my mistake is in deciding to read the book before going to the cinema. It's not that the film is better – it turns out to be a great adaptation that takes the basis of the book and turns it into an eminently watchable film – but it means that I already know what's going to happen. More than that, I know how the story is going to end before I finish reading it because of the picture section contained within the book.

It's impossible not to succumb to the temptation to flick through the pictures at some point, and as soon as I do, I discover what will unfold on the pages. Nevertheless, it remains an extraordinarily moving story that is all the more horrifying because it is true. And Dench and Coogan both deliver wonderful performances in the film. Steve Coogan seems to divide opinion, but whatever your feelings about him are, he's great in *Philomena*, just as he was brilliant in *The Trip*, the TV series he starred in alongside Rob Brydon that was both a gentle comedy and a work of genius.

Having already celebrated the beauty of the physical book with *The Luminaries*, I purchase another book that is, quite simply, stunning and just wouldn't work as an e-book. I'm talking about the exquisitely strange novel, *S*, a collaboration between the film producer J.J. Abrams and author Doug Dorst. It is described in reviews as a 'meta-fictional novel'. Apparently, 'meta-fiction' is the literary term describing fictional writing that self-consciously and systematically draws attention to its status as an artefact in posing questions about the relationship between fiction and reality, usually using irony and self-reflection. Not surprisingly, I have to look this up and if pressed, I would have to admit that I am struggling to understand the definition. I'm also finding it difficult to properly explain what *S* looks like or is about. J.J. Abrams attempts to shed light on his literary creation.

'You get a black slip case which has a seal on it which you break, and the book comes out, and the book looks like a 1949 library. When you open the book you discover that almost every page has writings in the margins in different colour inks and you realise that there are two people having a conversation – a play in a way that exists on top of this book, referencing the book, referencing each other and their lives. In fact, there are things that can't be said in the margins of the book, so there are things like letters that go into more detail about these people. There are

postcards that have very specific reasons for being in here and referencing certain things. There is a page from a college newspaper that talks about a flood that happened there... and one of my favourite pieces, which is this map that's on a napkin from the café at college. It's a brilliantly put together thing.'

I read about the book and then see a feature about it on the BBC *Newsnight* programme, and I know immediately that I'm going to buy it. That is the easy part. Once I get it, I'm actually scared to open it as if, somehow, I'm going to spoil it or 'break' it or ruin the magic of it. As I write these words, it still remains wrapped in its cellophane. I do like books that challenge or subvert our normal expectations of what a book is or should be – meta-fiction, I suppose – and I have a number of these in my possession.

The Unfortunates by B.S. Johnson is one such example. First published in the 1960s, this innovative 'book' comes within a box and consists of a first and last section plus twenty-five other chapters, each one presented as a self-contained pamphlet that can be read in any order the reader likes. I have neither read them chronologically nor in order.

In a similar vein, Tank Magazine brought out a series of books shaped as cigarette packets. The six books are: Joseph Conrad's *Heart of Darkness*; Ernest Hemingway's *The Undefeated* and *The Snows of Kilimanjaro*; Franz Kafka's *The Metamorphosis* and *In the Penal Colony*; Rudyard Kipling's *The Man Who Would Be King, The Phantom Rickshaw* and *Black Jack*; Robert Louis Stevenson's *Dr. Jekyll and Mr. Hyde*; Leo Tolstoy's *The Death of Ivan Ilych* and *Father Sergius*. At the time of their release, I still smoked, which was perhaps part of their appeal. These 'cigarette packet' books also remain behind their wrappings in pristine condition. If I reach that magical seventy years of age, maybe I should open a packet and read a book rather than smoke cigarettes? I'm still getting the *Playboy*, however.

Asking people you know to read your book, or manuscript, is either fraught with potential difficulties, or can be a waste of time. You might ask for honesty, but too much of it could see the end of beautiful friendships, while obligatory lavish praise gives you no indication as to whether your book is any good or not. Similarly, reading a friend's book poses the same problems for me. It's easy enough if I like it, or at least don't dislike it. Then, I can conjure up a myriad of meaningless praise. However, what if I don't like it? Do I say nothing? Do I say something? Do I just never get in touch with the person ever again?

I have these dilemmas as I start reading *The Birds That Never Flew* by Margot McCuaig. Margot is a friend of mine who I first met at Celtic when we worked together in the multi-media department; she's now gone on to bigger and better things, co-owning one television production company and being managing director of another ... and she's written a novel. How are there enough days in the week to do so many things?

In the dim and distant past, when we were work colleagues, we'd talk about our respective literary ambitions, with both of us expressing a desire to write and publish a novel. That we've both finally managed to achieve this is, to me, remarkable in itself, and in a month when another former Celtic colleague, Stephen Sullivan, publishes a biography of Sean Fallon – a legendary figure in the club's history – it's clear that a little bit of writing talent has flown through Celtic Park in recent years.

Thankfully, *The Birds That Never Flew* turns out to be a really good book which tells a powerful and sometimes shocking story of sexual abuse and domestic violence, primarily told through the life of Elizabeth, the main character in the novel. The subject matter is a difficult one, but it's handled really well – stark and sensitive at the same time – and there are even moments of real humour in the book, not least in the gallus Glasgow patter of the Virgin Mary. I'm not offering any further explanation for that. You'll have to read the book yourself. There are some stunning set-piece (and violent) moments, and occasionally I wonder whether there should be an 'All Men Are Bastards' sticker on the front cover, but I find myself thinking about Elizabeth after I'd finished *The Birds That Never Flew* and hoping that she'll be okay, and that's the mark of a really good novel.

My friend, Stevie Maule, and I occasionally meet for lunch, and on our most recent get-together, there is an exchange of books. I give him *The Road To Lisbon*, a wonderful football novel by Martin Greig and Charles McGarry which is centred around Celtic's European Cup triumph of 1967. Football novels are pretty thin on the ground, and good ones are even harder to find. *The Road To Lisbon* is up there amongst the very best. Stevie hands over a copy of *Q* by Luther Blissett. For starters, it's the second novel now in my possession that has a single letter as a title. Originally published in Italian, *Q* is set in Europe in the sixteenth century during the Reformation which is sweeping across the continent. Any football fans reading these words will recognise the name 'Luther Blissett'. He was a striker who played for Watford in the 1970s and '80s and, who, somewhat bizarrely, spent a year with AC Milan in Italy. His name is the nom de plume for the four Italian authors of the novel.

Once I start reading *Q*, I'm glad that I'd recently watched a two-part documentary about Martin Luther, because it gives me a basic understanding of what is going on in the novel. Just as when I read *Wolf Hall*, it reinforces the importance of the new innovation that was the printing press to help fuel the Reformation. There are possible parallels with the importance of social media to the Arab Spring of more recent times.

One Sunday I find myself in Glasgow city-centre on a rare shopping trip, and after quickly getting what my presence is required for, I leave Karen to continue shopping while I head for Waterstone's. I locate a copy of *Q* and, finding a spare armchair, open the book up at the chapter I've reached at home and read it until it's time to meet Karen. Despite this, however, *Q* is another book that I get bogged down in, and while I give up after eighty-four pages, I'm reluctant to admit this to Stevie, like it will be a confession of failure and he will think a little less of me. So I take the coward's way out and, having not told him I'd started the book, I don't confess to him that I've given up. Instead, I decide just to mention it here on these pages and break the news to him gently in this way. Sorry, Stevie!

I turn instead to *The Book of Lost Things* by John Connolly. It is clever, fascinating and absolutely absorbing to read. It tells the story of David, a twelve-year-old boy who is struggling to cope with the death of his mother, and then his father's subsequent re-marriage and the arrival on the scene of a new baby brother. The book is set just as the Second World War begins, which causes further upheaval in David's life, and he takes refuge in books, in particular myths and fairy tales. When a plane crashes into his back garden, David is propelled into a strange world that appears to be the creation of his own imagination, and he must try to find his way to the King who, in possession of the fabled Book of Lost Things, will be able to help him return home.

It is a book that is inspired by traditional fairy tales, but distorts them in disturbing and grotesque ways. This might be a novel about children and the power of books to fire their imagination, but it's not really a book for children. Much of the narrative is quite violent, which would certainly give children nightmares. I found it to be a captivating read, enhanced by an appendix that includes explanations of how the book was inspired by traditional myths and fairy tales, as well as detailing what they are and what their origins are. The author, John Connolly, writes.

'Originally much of it was written for a website that was created to complement the book, but the purpose of it was still the same: I wanted to give people the opportunity to delve further, if they chose, into the background not only of the novel, but of the original fairy tales that were used to create it. They're all quite fascinating in their own way, and I've argued elsewhere that we have a tendency, particularly in adulthood, to be rather dismissive of such tales. While The Book of Lost Things makes a

case for them, the notes gave me the chance to explore their origins, and their themes, more explicitly and in greater detail.

I also wanted to provide a resource for readers who found that the book had raised questions in their minds, or who wanted to discuss it with other readers. I'm interested in finding ways to expand upon the experience of reading a book. Those of us who love reading know that the experience doesn't end when we close the covers. Books linger. They plant seeds in our imaginations. That's the great joy of them. I suppose that's why I'm so enthusiastic about book groups, and much of the additional material was written with book groups in mind.'

As the end of November approaches, the Scottish government publishes their White Paper on what an independent Scotland would mean. Entitled, *'Scotland's Future: Your Guide to an Independent Scotland'*, the document aims to persuade people to vote 'Yes' in the 2014 referendum, explaining in great detail across a whole range of issues, why independence would be good for Scotland and Scots, and how it would impact on their lives. Not surprisingly, critics dismiss it as 'a work of fiction', but the wise words of Saint Thomas Aquinas spring to mind.

'To one who has faith, no explanation is necessary. To one without faith, no explanation is possible.'

I download the document on to my Kindle with the aim of reading it over the next few months. At a mere six hundred and seventy pages, it should be a breeze after having successfully read *The Luminaries*. While I don't need to be convinced about the merits – moral, emotional and practical – of an independent Scotland – I'm hoping the White Paper will provide me with further arguments to give to those who are still undecided or misguided.

The end of November also sees a celebration of Scottish literature, an important part of our culture and identity, as Scotland's favourite book of the past fifty years is announced. Organised by the Scottish Book Trust, it relies on a public vote, which, if the example of similar musical polls are any indication, will mean that something published in the past couple of years will come out on top since it's in the current consciousness of the public, rather than a novel published a few years ago. Thankfully, our book-reading nation is a little bit more discerning and opts for something published twenty years ago – *Trainspotting* by Irvine Welsh. My own personal favourite on the shortlist is Alasdair Gray's *Lanark*, which is not only a stunning Scottish novel, but deserves to be recognised as a great novel throughout the world. It's also a pivotal publication in the development of Scottish literature and its influence cannot be underestimated.

A few years back, during one of those phases in my life when I was worrying that my brain was no longer being exercised, I signed up for two, ten-week courses on twentieth-century Scottish literature at the University of Glasgow. The courses were brilliant, helped in no small part by a young and enthusiastic tutor who evidently knew his subject and, more importantly, loved it. We would be tasked with reading a book in the week leading up to the class and then there would be a discussion about it. If you hadn't managed to finish the book before the class, then the ending would be spoiled for you, since the entire novel was up for discussion. *Lanark*, naturally, was one of the novels featured in the course – we actually spent two weeks discussing it – and it definitely helped in my enjoyment and understanding of the book to be able to talk about it.

Alasdair Gray is also an extraordinary character, and if you get a chance to go and hear him speak about his writing, don't pass it up. It is an unforgettable experience. I actually once had the pleasure, surreal at times though it was, of taking him and his wife to dinner when the *Celtic View* commissioned him to design a special front cover of the magazine to commemorate our first participation in the group stages of the UEFA Champions League back in 2001. If you don't like football, I may have lost you at this point. It remains one of the most interesting and strange experiences of my time at Celtic. The magazine cover remains one of my favourites.

If you want to read the best Scottish novel ever, in my humble opinion, pick up a copy of *The Cone Gatherers* by Robin Jenkins. It was published in 1955, so didn't qualify for this latest poll, but it is magnificent, majestic and a masterpiece. *(See Appendix II)*

The end of November, the twenty-ninth to be precise, sees Glasgow hit by a terrible tragedy when a police helicopter crashes through the roof of the Clutha Bar, a busy city pub, on a Friday night. Ten people are killed in the accident and a city is in mourning. I have already admitted to loving Glasgow more than any other city on earth – and I know I haven't visited that many – but it is where I live and home is where the heart is. The instant reaction of Glaswegians to the accident not only reinforces my love of the city but also shows the world that the 'dear green place' is not a bad wee city to live in. London-based media outlets quickly wonder why, in this age of mobile phones and social media, there isn't more footage of the pub in the immediate aftermath of the helicopter crash. As a Scottish journalist points out, that's because Glaswegians were too busy rushing towards the pub and into it to help people rather than stopping to get out their phones and film events unfolding.

It's The Most Wonderful
Time Of The Year

*'I've always loved to read, but sometimes I go for a whole year
without reading because I forget to.'*

Norah Jones

December begins and I feel like I'm in the home straight of a
race that began away back in the dim and distant past –
Boxing Day, 2012 to be precise. There are a mere thirty-one
days left until my 'year of falling in love with literature again'
draws to a close. I should add that the sound of the cannon
atop Edinburgh Castle signalling the start of a new year will
not also herald the end of this relationship. I just won't be
writing another book about my reading habits of 2014.
However, just like a runner who sees the finishing line, I'm
imbued with a renewed sense of urgency and enthusiasm as I
enter December.

There is also great news with the announcement that
William McIlvanney's *Laidlaw* books are to be adapted for
television. I've read two out of three so far and both of them
are magnificent. McIlvanney had explained at the event I'd
attended earlier in the year that his character had been ripped
off and turned into the TV detective *Taggart*. Now, with the
resurgence in popularity of the *Laidlaw* trilogy, McIlvanney's
Glasgow detective is set to make the switch from the page to
the small screen. I don't want to get my hopes up, given that
discovering these books has been one of my literary
highlights of the past year, but as long as it's better than
Taggart, then I'll be happy. That shouldn't be too hard to
achieve.

I've started reading another non-fiction book, one of the
few football books I've read purely for pleasure this year, and

what a pleasure it is. Graham Hunter's book, *Spain: The Inside Story of La Roja's Historic Treble*, tells the story of the Spanish national football team and their unique success in winning three consecutive football tournaments – the European Championship in 2008, the World Cup in 2010, and the Euros again in 2012. Hunter, a Scottish journalist based in Barcelona, has enjoyed unique access to the Spanish squad, partly through his work with football's two main governing bodies, UEFA and FIFA, and so is in a perfect position to tell this fantastic sporting story. That he achieves what he sets out to do is due in no small part to his talent as a writer. It is an utterly captivating book and it's with real reluctance whenever I have to put it down.

It helps, too, that I go to see him at an event in the Glasgow Film Theatre to launch the book. He talks as well as he writes – he's already written a best-selling book about FC Barcelona's success – and the fact that over three hundred people turn up for the event is testimony to that. It may come across as a slightly tenuous link but it is while reading Graham Hunter's book that news of Nelson Mandela's death breaks. The tenuous link comes from the fact that one of the last public appearances the former South African president made was at the 2010 World Cup final in Johannesburg when Spain beat Holland to become world champions.

There is almost universal praise for Mandela, as a man of principle, who spent twenty-seven years in prison as a result of opposing South Africa's apartheid regime, and who then showed remarkable forgiveness when he was released in 1990, ensuring that the country's transition did not descend into chaos. Glasgow was one of the first places in the world to actively support and campaign for Mandela's release, with the council renaming part of the city-centre 'Nelson Mandela Place' in 1986, also granting him the freedom of the city, even as his own country was denying him his basic freedom. Three years after his release, in October 1993, Nelson Mandela visited Glasgow to say thank-you for the support he'd received while in captivity. He told the city:

'While we were physically denied our freedom in the country of our birth, a city 6,000 miles away, and as renowned as Glasgow, refused to accept the legitimacy of the apartheid system, and declared us to be free.'

There is also some literary news about a book which has made the England football manager, Roy Hodgson, and I kindred spirits. *Stoner* by John Williams has been named Waterstone's Book of the Year. It's been dubbed 'Lazarus Literature' because the book rose from the grave to become a best-seller, and credit for its success must surely go to the marketing department of Vintage Books whose campaign on behalf of *Stoner* is a blueprint for other publishers on how to do it. I'm not convinced that it merits the 'Book of the Year' award, though it does also give me hope that, at some unknown moment in the future, one of my novels will make a similarly miraculous resurrection and be lavished with praise and awards.

At the start of December, I'd toyed with the idea of just reading Christmas books to get into the festive mood – Ho! Ho! Ho! and all that – and the natural one to start with would be *A Christmas Carol* by Charles Dickens. I'm sure that many of you will have already read it, or at least be familiar with the story, but for some reason it's one of those books that I've struggled with, even though it's not a long or particularly 'heavy' book. I am going to read it, but I'll wait until Christmas week. For now, I start another novel, *Mr Penumbra's 24-hour Bookstore* by Robert Sloan, and I am so glad I make that decision.

It's a magical novel that is, in some ways, a book about books, just as *Read All About It* is as well. It celebrates books, and the enduring mystery and wonder of reading. Yet, it's also about the future of publishing and whether modern technology could be a positive influence on books and readers. The novel is a mystery, the mystery being what is the secret behind the façade of Mr Penumbra's 24-hour Bookshop and all the books hidden in its dark recesses, only to be allowed out to a select band of 'members'. This is no ordinary library but something altogether more secretive and sinister.

I start reading the book on a plane to Barcelona and I have a vague sense of guilt that I'm cheating on Oliver Potzsch since I'd been reading his books during two previous trips abroad this year. However, I quickly shrug off that feeling as I immerse myself in the enigma of *Mr Penumbra's 24-hour Bookstore*. I'm amazed at how much of the book I devour by the time the plane touches down in the capital of Catalonia.

I'm in Barcelona for Celtic's UEFA Champions League tie in the Nou Camp, and the first stop on Tuesday night is the stadium. It has a capacity of nearly one hundred thousand, and I've been lucky enough to have attended a game there when it's been almost full. However, there is something breathtaking about stepping into an empty sporting arena of this magnitude. The history of the club hangs in the air ... the screams and shouts of countless Catalans who have filed through the turnstiles over many years, mainly to support their team but sometimes to declare publicly, even just by their presence, pride in their 'national' identity, which is distinctive and definitely not Spanish. The ghosts of the great players who have graced this arena dance for all eternity under the adoring gaze of the floodlights while the presence of the current team lurks in the shadows, ready to be brought to life on a match day or night.

From the dressing rooms, there is a long staircase down towards what seems like a hole in the ground out of which the players emerge on to the pitch. Halfway down these steps on the right-hand side is a small chapel and I take the opportunity to visit for a few minutes of solitary prayer. It has been a while since I've had a moment like this and I'm glad that my rosary beads have remained a constant companion despite my ongoing crisis of faith.

The following day I visit the Sagrada Familia, the cathedral designed by Antoni Gaudi which was started in 1882 and is still not finished. It is a spectacular structure and, again, I sit inside for a few minutes of quiet contemplation – or as quiet as it's possible to be when there is a steady stream of chattering tourists pouring through the door, snapping away at every aspect of the spectacular architecture.

I don't pray for a Celtic victory. For one thing, I've learned over the years that God never answers that prayer, and even if that's what I'd offered up my prayers for, they go unheeded as Celtic lose 6-1. I actually bump into Graham Hunter in the press box at the stadium ahead of the game and take the opportunity to compliment him on his excellent *Spain* book.

When I come home from Barcelona in the early hours of Thursday morning, I discover that a bookcase has appeared in the small downstairs toilet in our house. It is as if my prayers, as vague and general as they were, really have been answered. God has looked into my heart and given me what He knows will make me happiest. The bookcase, in reality, is actually wallpaper covering one wall of the toilet but its sepia-tone image of books makes me smile. I could thank God, but it's actually Karen's idea so she deserves my gratitude.

It doesn't take me long to finish *Mr Penumbra's 24-hour Bookstore*. It remains a magical tale that definitely extols the virtue of books while suggesting that modern technology – whatever that might have been through the ages – will always be a potential threat to books, though at the same time it can often be their biggest ally, which is an idea worth bearing in mind during this continuous debate between physical books and e-books. It's not too surprising to discover, after I've finished the book, that Robert Sloan once worked for Twitter, which has given him a unique and, at the same time, balanced perspective on the issue.

I return to William McIlvanney's 'Laidlaw' books and the final part of the trilogy, *Strange Loyalties*. McIlvanney is, quite simply, a magnificent writer. Have I told you that at some point already during this journey we've been on? Once you finish this book, and there's not too long to go now, go out and buy the *Laidlaw* trilogy. If you've already got the books, then buy a set for a friend. They will thank you for the gift. The novels are so much more than simply crime stories. They represent astute and precise character studies, while the writing is incisive and addictive. *Strange Loyalties* is as much a novel about Laidlaw and how he deals with the sudden death of his brother in a road accident as it is about his life and work as a policeman.

It's also at this point that I happen to stumble upon a new word one Sunday night when the *X-Factor* programme makes a rare and unwelcome appearance on my TV. One of the judges, Nicole Scherzinger, describes a performance by one of the acts as 'shamazing'. At first I think I've misheard so I rewind and listen again. Sure enough, she has said it. As with most instances when something puzzling presents itself, I take to Google for the answer. The definition, according to an online Urban Dictionary, reads:

> *Shamazing: An adjective to describe something that is more than just amazing.*
> *eg: Nance and Donald are so shamazing because they are beautiful, smart, hilarious, and lactate beer from their nipples.*

Can you sense a rant coming on? Can you? It's definitely coming. It's like watching the glass of water in *Jurassic Park* beginning to quiver as the Tyrannosaurus Rex gets ever closer. Count to ten, Paul. Count to ten ... and then count again ... and again ... and again ... and again ...

I take to Twitter to reveal that I am unimpressed at the discovery of this strange new non-word and a friend of mine, Jamie Kerr, dares me to use 'shamazing' in my next book, promising to buy ten copies of the book if I do. He'll be surprised, and shamazed, to discover that I've managed to do just that. At least I know that I've sold ten copies of *Read All About It*, if nothing else. Incidentally, the song in question from the *X-Factor* is anything but shamazing, although I have to say that Nicole Scherzinger most definitely is.

Having finished *Strange Loyalties*, and now finding myself in a dilemma as to what my favourite literary trilogy is between McIlvanney, Richard Ford or Cormac McCarthy – all other suggestions gratefully received – I decide that it is beginning to feel a lot like Christmas and so psyche myself up to tackle *A Christmas Carol* again. At the same time, on December 18, a new book magically appears on my Kindle. I had pre-ordered Daniela Sacerdoti's novel, *Take Me Home*, about a month ago and when I switch on the Kindle on publication day, it is there waiting for me to read, which I am going to do once I have dispensed with Ebenezer Scrooge. I'm looking forward to reading it, given that her previous novel, *Watch Over Me*, was wonderful. When I say her previous novel, I'm doing Daniela a disservice. Not only is she talented, but she has a prodigious output, having written books for children, young adults and adults – seven in total to date – and I remain very impressed by the quality and quantity of her writing, while slightly guilty at the paucity of mine.

Even as Christmas gets ever closer, I have to admit that I take little part in the collective madness that descends upon the world. Any presents that you may receive from the Cuddihys come courtesy of Karen. She even buys her own presents from me as well. Yes, I am hanging my head in shame as I make this confession. This year, I do think about making a small contribution by giving everyone a book. It's always a good present to receive – well, I think so anyway – and it fits in nicely with this literary journey I've been on throughout 2013. I had thought of doing it last year – not necessarily buying them but taking books from my collection. In the end I didn't. At the moment, it's just a thought, particularly since it would mean giving away books, something I'm generally reluctant to do.

I also have to confess that I do possess a modicum of arrogance when it comes to deciding which book to give a particular person. I think I have good literary tastes, and so presume my gift will be a welcome and appropriate one. The other side of this coin is that I prefer to receive a book token. It means I can go and buy books that I actually want to read.

It all stems from Christmases past when my parents – I suspect it was my mum – bought me books that I would be loathe even to use as a door-stop. It wasn't intentional on their part, I hasten to add. The principle of buying books for your children is a good one, and Santa always gave me and my sisters books every year, but when I was given *Spycatcher* by Peter Wright back in the late 1980s, I decided I had to take a stand and tell my parents I wasn't going to read it, and that I hadn't read the 'best sellers' they'd bought me in previous years. From then on, I've received a book token, which some of you may think is far too generous a gift for someone who sounds like an ungrateful teenager, but it's an arrangement that seems to keep everyone happy – well, me really – so don't rock the boat by saying anything.

At the third time of asking I manage to complete *A Christmas Carol*. It is one to tick off as having read, but like a lot of Christmas-themed stories, whether they are in book form or, in more recent years, cinematic format, it is a bit simplistic and saccharine in its message. I love Charles Dickens, and I'm glad to have read one of his books during this past year, although I wish it was something else like *Bleak House*, which I've been wanting to read for a while now.

My intention, on finishing *A Christmas Carol* a couple of days before Christmas – my daughter, Louise's twenty-sixth birthday – is to switch to the Kindle and tackle Daniela Sacedoti's new novel. Before then, however, I delve briefly into a new short story collection written by a friend of mine, Andy Reilly. The book, *The Glasgow Underground & Nicotine*, has eleven Glasgow-based stories, each title a play on a Velvet Underground song. While I will take more time to read the whole collection, I can't resist reading *'All Jo Morrow's Panties'*. The title, for those of you in need of an explanation, is a play on the song *'All Tomorrow's Parties'*. The author deserves praise for the title alone – and I am a big admirer of anyone who comes up with great titles – while the story itself is a small piece of Glasgow humour that is written in the best possible taste. It augurs well for the rest of the collection.

I haven't used my Kindle much this year, outwith the times we've been on holiday, but I make an exception to read *Take Me Home* by Daniela Sacerdoti. This is due to the fact that the e-book is released this month while the physical version isn't published until April 2014. It's an unusual strategy from Black & White Publishing, and it will be interesting to find out what impact this has on sales of the physical book when it is released. Their decision may have something to do with the phenomenal success of Daniela's previous novel, *Watch Over Me*, which can boast of e-book sales approaching half a million. That is an incredible figure, and the publishers may simply be acknowledging the online audience which has been created.

Both that novel and the new book, *Take Me Home*, are set in the fictional village of Glen Avich in the Scottish Highlands. I would guess that both novels have a higher percentage of female readers, though I'm loathe to label either of them 'chick lit'. It's a lazy categorisation which might stop some of you reading the books, and while the elements of romance, drama and magic might seem, at a casual glance, to be aimed primarily at women, both novels are just extremely good stories. Daniela writes beautifully, which I admit with much admiration and not a little envy, and *Take Me Home*, a story of love, loss and never forgetting who you are and where you come from, is a book I can't put down, finishing it within three days of starting it.

I have also reached Boxing Day, and when I get up early in the morning ahead of a lunchtime drive to Perth for a Celtic game – I'm not driving, I hasten to add, since our Christmas Day festivities continued until four o'clock in the morning – two things come to mind. One is that I'm a lot brighter than I was twelve months ago. Whether it's because we hosted Christmas dinner this year, but I have consumed less alcohol and so feel better for it. The other is that memories of twelve months ago come flooding back as I realise it was on this day in 2012 that I resolved to read more books. I open the 'wardrobe' doors which conceal my ever-expanding collection of books, catching sight of just some of the books which have kept me company over the past year. It feels like an incredibly quick journey, like I should say out loud, 'The year's just flown in.' It's the sort of comment that will mark me out as getting old, in much the same way that every reluctant conversation that I have about the weather seems to confirm that I am turning into my dad.

It has been a quick year, and an enjoyable journey – for me, at least. I don't want to be presumptuous on your behalf. I have now reached the seventy-book mark for the year which, depending on your own reading proficiency, is either an impressive or a paltry total, and it's not finished yet.

Since I've reached exactly one year on from my starting point I could finish now, at least as far as this book is concerned, but I feel that, with five days left of 2013, I will be able to read one more 'bonus' book to bring this to a conclusion on the last day of the year. Christmas Day has come and gone without me either giving or receiving books, or even getting a book token from my parents. Perhaps my mum got wind of my disparaging comments regarding previous presents and decided to punish me accordingly?

There is one festive surprise which does arrive, courtesy of an email from my work colleague whose flat had been broken into back in August, with my Kindle amongst the burglar's swag. The email comes via Amazon and informs me that I have a fifty-pound gift voucher, along with a message from my colleague – I need to call him my friend now – that this is to acknowledge my loss. Well, now that I come to think of it, I was quite upset at the time. It is a lovely and a generous gesture, and an unexpected Christmas present for me.

So I am now in front of the proverbial blank canvas once again. What to read next? It seems appropriate that the last book I read in 2013 is one that isn't published until April 2014. The novel in question is *The Walk Home* by Rachel Seiffert, and it has been delivered to me at work along with a handwritten postcard.

'Dear Paul Cuddihy – Rachel Seiffert requested me to send you a copy of her new novel, to be published in April, with her best wishes. Thanks, Zoe Hood.'

I am thrilled, delighted and not a little surprised. I had contact with Rachel a few years ago at a time when the *Celtic View* was publishing short stories every month from new and established writers. Rachel was very keen to write something for us but due to various reasons – work and family commitments – it never came to pass. So I am touched that she has thought to send me her new novel, allowing me to read it months before everyone else. The novel is set in Glasgow, and there is much about the story that is entrenched in the city of the past and the present, but it's also a book which examines family life – the ties that bind, sometimes oppressively so, and what happens when those ties are undone.

I love the book because it is about my city, and also because it's so well-written. The characters are recognisable and real, some of them appealing and some of them less so, but still engaging nevertheless. If I'm being honest, part of the appeal of *The Walk Home* is feeling that I'm in a privileged position of getting to read the preview copy so that I can bore people over the next few months by telling them how good it is and that they should buy it when it's published. This doesn't happen to me very often – ever – so please indulge me in this instance.

I finish Rachel Seiffert's book in the early hours of December 31 and wake up on Hogmanay with a (small) sense of achievement. I am the man of a million ideas, none of which ever seem to come to fruition, and so to have set myself this task and seen it through represents a breakthrough for me. I decide to give myself the day off from reading. After seventy-one books, I feel like I deserve a day of watching television and eating chocolates. I'll start again tomorrow, which is another year altogether.

Conclusion

'A person who publishes a book wilfully appears before the populace with his pants down. If it is a good book nothing can hurt him. If it is a bad book nothing can help him.'

Edna St Vincent Millay

So we've finally arrived at the end of our journey and in committing my experience to the printed page, I am now standing before you with my metaphorical pants at my ankles. It's not a pretty image, is it?

It seems so long ago since we began, with me staring at my book-shelves and resolving to read more books. I have read seventy-one books in the course of this journey which has lasted three hundred and seventy-one days. That works out at a book every 5.22 days which, to me, is fairly impressive. You may also be suitably impressed, or you might be completely underwhelmed by the total. There's no need to tell me, however. Be content with the knowledge that you're better than me. When I consider the other books I've had to read for work, and also as research for my Booker Prize-winning novel yet to be written, then I know I could improve upon that total. Maybe I will in the twelve months ahead, though that's something you'll never hear about.

I can only speak for myself when I say that I've enjoyed every minute of this literary adventure, more or less. There have only been a few books which I've abandoned without finishing, and I don't feel guilty at all for having done so. More importantly, I've read some wonderful books, loads of them, in fact, and looking back over my full reading list, it's difficult to choose my favourites. There have been so many.

I'm glad that I've now read William McIlvanney's *Laidlaw* trilogy. It makes me proud that my small country can produce such a massive literary talent who deserves to be recognised on the global stage. In the same vein, finally getting the better of a James Kelman novel has represented a major achievement for me, and to come out the other side of *You Have To Be Careful In The Land Of The Free* with a real admiration for his skill as a novelist is a highlight of the year.

Another trilogy I enjoyed – during my partially successful 'trilogy month' – was Cormac McCarthy's *Border Trilogy*, though that merely confirmed what I already knew about McCarthy's ability as a writer. The downside of that month, and one of the most surprising and disappointing aspects of the year was my experience with Roddy Doyle's *Last Roundup* trilogy. On the other hand, Doyle's novel, *A Greyhound of a Girl*, would be among my favourite books that I've read if I was pushed to produce a list. It is a beautiful story and even if it is targeted at younger readers, it could only be the coldest of adult hearts that wouldn't warm to this book. A special mention also goes to David Walliams' *Billionaire Boy* for being a funny and uplifting tale.

Reading the Booker Prize shortlist was another achievement for me, even though the judges didn't concur with my choice of winner. I still think I was right, incidentally. In saying that, the winning novel, *The Luminaries* by Eleanor Catton, was still a very worthy winner and it does represent everything that is wonderful and joyous about books. As a physical product, it is absolutely beautiful. I always felt I was holding something special in my hands whenever I picked it up and I had a real sense of achievement in managing to read all eight hundred and thirty-two pages.

Even before I started out on this literary journey, I was already in the camp that preferred actual books to virtual ones, and nothing I have read in the past twelve months has caused me to change my mind. I do own a Kindle which is now a regular holiday companion, but my year of falling in love with literature again has also confirmed my love of books as a physical product. That love, I know for sure now, will never die.

My main aim, in setting myself this challenge was to read

more, and I feel that I've more than achieved that goal. More importantly, having got back into the reading habit, I'm not about to let it drop in the year ahead. A book is now my regular companion, and even giving myself a day off on December 31 doesn't feel right. The other aim, as the months progressed, was to chronicle my efforts, and that I have also achieved. The jury is now out as to whether I have done so successfully.

In choosing to share my thoughts about the books I've read and which have kept me company over the past year in this book which I've published, I am, in the words of the American poet and playwright, Edna St Vincent Millay, wilfully appearing before the populace with my pants down. If I feel a little chilly and embarrassed at the prospect, I hope you enjoy this book enough to make me feel a little less uncomfortable.

Appendix I: The Reading List

December 26, 2012 – December 31, 2013

CHAPTER ONE: YOU SAY YOU WANT A RESOLUTION
December 26, 2012 – February 1, 2013

Diamonds Are Forever:	Ian Fleming
Scoop:	Evelyn Waugh
We Need To Talk About Kevin:	Lionel Shriver
The Plot Against America:	Philip Roth
Laidlaw:	William McIlvanney
The Bishop's Man:	Linden MacIntyre
The Code of the Woosters:	P.G. Wodehouse
When It Happens To You:	Molly Ringwald
A Study In Scarlet:	Arthur Conan Doyle

CHAPTER TWO: FROM STARKS PARK TO SEVENTH AVENUE
February 2 – March 2

Ride With The Devil:	Daniel Woodrell
Pride and Prejudice:	Jane Austen
Seventy Times Seven:	John Gordon Sinclair
The Hangman's Daughter:	Oliver Potzsch
Canada:	Richard Ford

CHAPTER THREE: SEEING IS BELIEVING
March 3 – April 5

The Vulture:	Gil Scott-Heron
Billionaire Boy:	David Walliams

CHAPTER FOUR: A KICK UP THE EIGHTIES
April 6 – April 27

CHAPTER FIVE: THREE IS A MAGIC NUMBER
April 28 – June 4

CHAPTER SIX: DO DO DO DO DODO, DO DO DO DO DODO
June 5 – June 28

When The Women Come
Out To Dance: Elmore Leonard

CHAPTER SEVEN: LAZING ON A SUNNY AFTERNOON
June 29 – July 31

The 100-year-old Man Who
Climbed Out Of A Window
And Disappeared: Jonas Jonasson
Disgrace: J.M. Coetzee
SS-GB: Len Deighton
The Beggar King: Oliver Potzsch
One Hundred Years of Solitude:Gabriel Garcia Marquez
Pandaemonium: Christopher Brookmyre
Wolf Hall: Hilary Mantel
The Yellow Birds: Kevin Powers

CHAPTER EIGHT: #CURMUDGEON
August 1 – September 9

Stoner: John Williams
The Knot: Mark Watson
The Finkler Question: Howard Jacobson
Ratlines: Stuart Neville
Brave New World: Aldous Huxley
The Imperfectionists: Tom Rachman

CHAPTER NINE: DON'T JUDGE A BOOKER BY ITS COVER
September 10 – October 13

We Need New Friends: NoViolet Bulawayo
The Luminaries: Eleanor Catton

Harvest: Jim Crace
The Lowland: Jhumpa Lahiri
A Tale for the Time Being: Ruth Oseki
The Testament of Mary: Colm Toibin

CHAPTER TEN: THERE'S MORE TO LIFE THAN BOOKS, BUT NOT MUCH MORE
October 14 – October 31

The Fire Gospel: Michael Faber
The Unlikely Pilgrimage
Of Harold Fry: Rachel Joyce
Morrissey: The Autobiography   Morrissey

CHAPTER ELEVEN: BASED ON A TRUE STORY
November 1 – November 30

Muckraker: W. Sydney Robinson
Philomena: Martin Sixsmith
The Birds That Never Flew: Margot McCuaig
The Book of Lost Things: John Connolly

CHAPTER TWELVE: IT'S THE MOST WONDERFUL TIME OF THE YEAR
December 1 – December 31

Spain: The Inside Story of
La Roja's Historic Treble: Graham Hunter
Mr Penumbra's 24-hour
Bookstore: Robin Sloan
Strange Loyalties: William McIlvanney
A Christmas Carol: Charles Dickens
Take Me Home: Daniela Sacerdoti
The Walk Home: Rachel Seiffert

Appendix II: Ten Of My Favourites

Having read a total of seventy-one books between December 26, 2012 and December 31, 2013, here are a further ten of my all-time favourites, which I would also recommend to everyone. I made an original list which included Richard Ford's *The Sportswriter*, but I decided to replace that with another title so you have ten new recommendations over and above the seventy-one I've read and written about, although I may have already mentioned some of them in passing.

The Grapes of Wrath: John Steinbeck

This is a beautiful and moving book with an ending that would make anyone cry – well, I had a tear or two in my eyes. It is actually one of the few books I've read which has had that effect on me. Everything about *The Grapes of Wrath* is perfect, and Steinbeck's writing is just incredible. Chronicling the journey of Americans in the 1930s from the dustbowl of Oklahoma to the 'promised land' of San Francisco, it is a stunning novel which is moving and harrowing, while Steinbeck's description of the food that is cooked and eaten on the road makes my mouth water. I can't recommend this book highly enough. Everyone should read this at least once in their life. I've read it three times.

The Cone Gatherers: Robin Jenkins

Scotland's greatest writer, and his greatest book. I would make it compulsory for this book to be taught in Scottish schools – I certainly wish we'd studied it when I was at school – as it would introduce a lot of people to the genius of Jenkins. He also wrote one of the best football novels I've ever read – *The Thistle and the Grail* – but *The Cone Gatherers* should be recognised, not just as a classic Scottish novel, but as a great novel. It tells the story of two conscientious

READ ALL ABOUT IT

objectors working on a Scottish estate during World War
Two, and Jenkins skilfully guides this dark and brooding tale
to its powerful conclusion. Another book I've read several
times, as well as gifting copies to friends and family over the
years.

Underworld: Don DeLillo

This is a mammoth and majestic novel with one of the best
opening sections of any book that I've ever read. *Underworld*
begins on October 3, 1951 at a famous baseball game in New
York. In the ninth inning of the game, Bobby Thomson hits a
three-run homer – use Google for an explanation of the rules
and terminology of baseball. It wins the game and the hit has
become known as 'the shot heard around the world', given
that US servicemen in various locations were listening to the
game on the radio. The whereabouts of the ball that
Thomson hit – while remaining a mystery in real life –
become a recurring theme throughout the novel. *Underworld* is
a magnificent story of America over four decades and weighs
in at a modest eight hundred and twenty-seven pages. It's
worth persevering with, though. Incidentally, Thomson was
born in Glasgow before his family emigrated to the United
States in the 1920s. I have a baseball signed by Bobby
Thomson which a friend bought for me. It's not the one he
hit back in 1951.

A Suitable Boy: Vikram Seth

This is a big book – as in one thousand, four hundred and
seventy-four pages, which makes it easily the longest novel
I've ever read – and I have to admit that I was a bit
intimidated when I first picked it up. In fact, I'm still amazed
that I actually read it, but it was one of the easiest and most
enjoyable books I've ever read. It's set in post-independence
India, and tells the story of a mother's search for a suitable
boy to marry her daughter. It's a wonderfully entertaining tale
which will keep you captivated from start to finish, and even
with a large cast of characters, you never lose sight of the

narrative (Russian novels, take note). Don't be put off by the size. It doesn't matter.

The Road: Cormac McCarthy

This book is simply incredible, one of the best books I have ever read. I mentioned it already, but it's worth reminding you. I couldn't put it down. It made me want to write something moving and meaningful though at the same time I realised I would never be able to produce anything that gets anywhere near that standard. And even though I thought the film adaptation was a fine one, it can't even begin to get close to the breathtaking perfection of the novel. Several copies have passed through my hands on their way to other people. I do slightly judge people on their reaction to *The Road*. I know I shouldn't.

The Three Musketeers: Alexandre Dumas

Dumas' classic novel of seventeenth century France is a swashbuckling adventure that I always find entertaining – it's another book that I've read several times – and it was certainly inspirational when it came to writing my own novel, *Saints and Sinners*. I think *The Three Musketeers* is the absolute benchmark for historical adventure novels and I find myself going back to it again and again. I'm still striving to reach that level, I hasten to add, having come nowhere near Dumas' brilliance in my own novels. There is a wonderful line in the TV series *Blackadder The Third* when Blackadder describes his novel, *Edmund: A Butler's Tale,* as 'a huge, rollercoaster of a novel in four hundred sizzling chapters; a searing indictment of domestic servitude in the eighteenth century, with some hot gypsies thrown in.' *The Three Musketeers* is even better than that!

Charlie & the Chocolate Factory: Roald Dahl

My favourite book from childhood, and I always wish I could find a Wonka Bar that tastes as good as how they sound in the book. *Charlie and the Chocolate Factory* is a wonderful tale and I even enjoyed both of the film versions. Roald Dahl is a masterful storyteller, and his books, while aimed at a younger readership can, and should, still appeal to adults. It was reading stories like *Charlie and the Chocolate Factory* when I was a child which made me fall in love with books. Incidentally, Nestle have recently introduced a selection of Wonka Bars with different centres. I would recommend the Millionaire's Shortbread one.

The Clan of the Cave Bear: Jean M. Auel

I read this book on holiday in Salou a few years ago and it blew me away. It's one of the few times I've read a book and been so absorbed and engrossed in it that I never wanted it to end. I can't remember why it had caught my eye in the book shop but it's an extraordinary feat of storytelling. Auel's novel goes back to the earliest days of human life on earth, when Homo sapiens and Neanderthals enjoyed an uneasy co-existence. It tells the story of a little girl, Ayla, who, following an earthquake, finds herself completely alone. She is taken in by a Neanderthal group and is brought up by them. *The Clan of the Cave Bear* is the first book in the brilliant Earth Children's series, and it remains my favourite. It's an unexpected treasure.

Me and Ma Gal: Des Dillon

A brilliant book by a brilliant Scottish writer. *Me and Ma Gal* is another book that should be taught in our schools and also heralded throughout the land. It's a brilliantly captivating novel that is funny at points and chillingly dark at other times. The novel charts a day in the life of the narrator, Derek, and his best friend, Gal, in their home town of Coatbridge, while a strange, unsettling and possibly psychopathic character roams about in the same woods where they play. Jack McConnell, Scotland's former First Minister, said of the book, 'If you didn't grow up in Scotland you will enjoy this book. But if you did grow up here you will absolutely love it.'

Oliver Twist: Charles Dickens

Every list of favourite books should include a novel by Charles Dickens because he is the master storyteller. It was a tough choice between *Oliver Twist*, *Great Expectations* and *A Tale of Two Cities*, but I've opted for *Oliver Twist* just because it was the first Dickens novel I read. I also like the way that, in Dickens' novels, characters ejaculate when they talk – not literally, of course. Although it's just a description of their speech, it does make me smile whenever I read it. Sorry, but sometimes I don't act my age. Most people will be familiar with the story of the eponymous Oliver, probably through seeing a film adaptation. The book is infinitely better. In saying that, I once saw a stage version of the story while on a visit to London, with Russ Abbot starring as Fagan. He was magnificent.

Appendix III: Other People's Favourites

So, enough about me ... I decided to ask a few people I know about the books that mean something to them. It could be their favourite book from childhood, or one that had an impact on them in adulthood. It might even be the last book they read. It's an eclectic choice of titles, much like the people themselves, and it's already given me a couple of ideas for future reading.

I really enjoyed Roddy Doyle's Barrytown trilogy. The humour in the books is brilliant, and I thought *The Snapper* in particular was hilarious. I remember being on a plane and laughing out loud while I was reading it, and that's not something which usually happens to me when I'm reading. The books were also turned into films – Colm Meaney plays the father in them – and you always worry that they'll not be as good, but I thought they were. I think it's the way the books are written, with most of it in dialogue that reads like it's already a film script. I also see that Roddy Doyle's writing Roy Keane's memoir and I'm looking forward to reading that. It sounds like an interesting partnership. In a similar way, I really enjoy Irvine Welsh's novels. He writes the way people speak and I think it makes the books better as a result.

NEIL LENNON, Manager, Celtic Football Club

The impact of reading *Treasure Island* at the age of seven or eight has never left me. It was exciting, intriguing and led me into another world. There have been varied claims about the effect of literature but Robert Louis Stevenson taught me early that a book offered an escape hatch to contentment. Thanks, Rab.

HUGH MacDONALD, sports writer

The novel I have enjoyed most is *The Chessmen* by Peter May, the third book in his Lewis Trilogy. I've enjoyed each of these books but *The Chessmen* – set in the Western Isles – is my favourite of the three. It is a great example of May's visual storytelling and tight plot. Peter May is one of Scotland's most successful screenwriters and all three novels are fantastic portrayals of contemporary life on the islands – highly evocative, descriptively rich and with well-drawn characters. My only regret is that having finished *The Chessmen,* the trilogy, too, has come to an end. I am jealous of readers who have still to start these wonderful books from the beginning.

NICOLA STURGEON, Deputy First Minister of Scotland

Heart of a Dog by Mikael Bulgakov is everything a book should be: short, funny and life-changingly astute. Told from a stray dog's point of view, the story is set in Moscow shortly after the Russian Revolution. A professor takes the dog in and operates on him, giving him the pituitary gland and testicles of a man who died in a knife fight. The dog turns into a quasi human, starts to demand housing, makes political speeches about his rights and gets a job as a cat strangler. The professor gives him a second operation to turn him back into a dog. It's one of the first books I ever read seriously and it's still an inspiration.

DENISE MINA, writer

The Private Memoirs and Confessions of a Justified Sinner by James Hogg is a book that both fired my imagination and chilled my soul. I was an 18-year-old student when I first read it and it staggered me in every possible way. Written in 1824, Hogg's exposition of mental breakdown – a towering, ground-breaking achievement in itself – is interlinked with supernatural themes that literally send shivers down the spine. It is also a searing commentary on religious fanaticism – with Calvin its main target – which is as relevant today as it was

then. Hogg's work has echoed through Scottish literature, influencing the likes of Robert Louis Stevenson, Muriel Spark and Alasdair Gray. Strangely, for a book which impacted me more than any other, I have only ever read it once. I have tried to return to it many times over the years, but it is like a strange world which I was only able to fully inhabit once.
MARTIN GREIG, author & publisher

It has to be *Don Quixote*. That sounds like a poncey, show-offy choice, but I have good reasons ... It's arguably the first novel ever – its 400th anniversary is 2015. How many books are still genuinely funny (and then genuinely heart-breaking) nearly half a millennia after publication? (Shakespeare isn't funny now. When your English teacher laughed out loud at *Much Ado*, she/he was just showing off and being poncey). But *Quixote* is also perfect for *this* book, seeing as how it's about a man whose life was transformed and made fun, but also totally screwed up by books.
CHRIS DOLAN, writer

The book I choose is *The Lord Of The Rings*. I have lovely memories of this book because my dad used to read it to me. It excited me and scared me and gave me a sense of wanting to see beyond this world and this reality. It was a big influence on me as a person and as a writer.
DANIELA SACERDOTI, novelist & scriptwriter

I was a spotty teenager with more hang-ups than a call-centre when I first read *Portnoy's Complaint* (1969) by Philip Roth. I hadn't yet read *Catch 22* or *Herzog* so I didn't know about the other brilliant Jewish American writers who were waiting to be discovered. *Portnoy's Complaint* was frank, fearless and funny as hell. Like most boys I discovered my sexuality in the bathroom and looked set to become the blind arm-wrestling champion of the West of Scotland. Alexander Portnoy's journey from adolescence to adulthood captures perfectly all the things you can't speak to anybody about at that age. It let me laugh out loud at things that would otherwise be met with embarrassed silence. I think it's still probably the dirtiest and funniest book I've read. But it's much more than that: it's about guilt and growing up, about being old before your time. Like Heller's *Something Happened*, it gave me the sense of a writer looking back on a period of his life like the one I was passing through and sharing both the hurt and hilarity of that time, and also the bittersweet fruits of wisdom that come with the backward look.

WILLY MALEY, university professor

I have just finished reading *When I Heard the Bell* by John MacLeod, the account of the wreck of the Iolaire in the early hours of New Year's Day 1919. On board, sailing home to the Isle of Lewis, were 284 men who had served in the First World War, some of them since the start of the conflict. With its captain sleeping below and on the bridge an inexperienced junior who, on a night of mist and drizzle, confused the lights which should have guided him into Stornoway, the vessel crashed into rocks known as the Beasts of Holm and foundered at the mouth of the harbour. Within yards of their native shore, in the worst peacetime disaster in British waters and the worst British maritime loss of life in peacetime since the Titanic, 205 men drowned – only 79 survived. Almost 7,000 Lewis men had served in the war, and nearly 1,000 had been killed. The additional loss of so many who had come through the conflict reverberated for generations. Perhaps the most extraordinary feature of the disaster is that it is virtually unknown in Scotland – another source of hurt for Lewis. To put it in perspective, the death toll in the Tay Bridge Disaster was 60. What other country would ignore its history in such fashion? And now I'm reading *Collected Stories*, by Bernard MacLaverty. He is a neighbour and friend and it has been a particular pleasure to hear him read aloud 'On the Roundabout', a poignant but amusing account of a violent incident during The Troubles in his native Northern Ireland.

RODDY FORSYTH, journalist & broadcaster

I had just got into U2's music at the age of about 20 when I found myself exploring the more experimental rock music ... Enter *Achtung Baby* into my life. The album was 10 years old by then but I hadn't heard it first time around over the noise of Kurt Cobain's angst and the Gallagher brothers' arguments. The mix of U2's sound with the technology of dance music made it an exciting album to explore. Apparently, back in the 1990s its impact had been felt worldwide and this is when Bill Flanagan, a New York Irish writer, spent two years inside the 'U2 bubble' on tour, in the studio, social engagements and behind the scenes in clubs and hotels. They said to him that anything he heard them say was fair game; it would be a 'warts and all' account, which is what the book, *U2 At The End Of The World,* is. He joins them as they embark on the ZooTV tour, a spectacular worldwide audio-visual extravaganza. They meet Bill Clinton, participate in a Greenpeace mission, invite Salman Rushdie out of hiding to join them on stage. They do a regular live satellite link-up to an underground bunker in Sarajevo to highlight the war there when the world was turning its back and, amongst all of that, they manage to do some huge ground-breaking gigs and actually go back into the studio to record the *Zooropa* album. I have never read a book that brings the reader so far inside the world of such a huge band and, believe me, I have searched for similar books on other bands – they just don't exist. It seems it is as unique a book as U2 are a band and we, the readers, get the closest thing to experiencing it all in person as we are ever likely to get. A truly remarkable book.

RONAN MacMANUS, songwriter & musician,
The BibleCode Sundays

The Descent of Woman by Elaine Morgan (1972) was life-changing for me. It brought together ideas about sociology, physiology, feminism and politics and was an accessible introduction to evolutionary theory. All of this before Richard Dawkins had published *The Selfish Gene.* Suddenly a whole lot of things made sense. I particularly

loved the way Morgan crossed academic boundaries. An Arts graduate, she decided to take on the scientific consensus after reading a 1960 article on an 'Aquatic Ape Hypothesis' of human evolution: the idea that our ancestors' most significant evolutionary changes came about not on the savannah, but when they were forced to adapt to a marine environment. She explained how this could account for many of the unsolved mysteries of human evolution. Scientists treated it with scorn but she ignored the criticism and went on to write several more fascinating books on the subject. Her theory has finally acquired some scientific currency in recent years. I wrote to congratulate her in 2010 and her modest response was: 'I'm glad I lived long enough to see the savannah theory bite the dust! It wasn't any arguments of mine that convinced them, it was their own improved techniques, but that doesn't matter.'
DINI POWER, English teacher

I re-read James Hogg's *The Private Memoirs and Confessions of a Justified Sinner* every couple of years. The novel defies summarising, but its themes of duality and hypocrisy are as relevant today as when Hogg first published the book in 1824. Duality is everywhere in *Confessions*. Doubleness stalks the plot and underpins the novel's structure and language. *The Private Memoirs and Confessions of a Justified Sinner* also helped birth Robert Louis Stevenson's *The Strange Case of Dr Jekyll and Mr Hyde*. That alone would make it a book to be admired, but Hoggs' novel is a playful, inventive, challenging read, as slippery and shape-changing as its anti-hero Gil-Martin.
LOUISE WELSH, writer

ACKNOWLEDGEMENTS

There are so many people to thank in relation to this book ... wait a minute, it's just a book about my year of reading more books and then writing about it, so really, all the thanks should go to me.

All poor jokes aside, my friend of many years, Stevie Maule, remains one of my biggest supporters and continues to offer vital encouragement at every turn ... as well as a few free lunches. I am, as always, very grateful; the encouragement is appreciated too.

For the wonderful cover design, and all her patience in making every requested amendment, my thanks go to Siobhann Caulfield, and to Joe Sullivan for casting an expert eye over the manuscript.

I'm indebted to the advice of my friend and fellow writer, Andy Reilly, who also showed great patience in answering all my (daft) questions and helping to guide me through this publishing malarkey.

I would also like to thank Chris Dolan, Martin Greig and Hugh MacDonald for their support and advice at every turn. If I have missed anyone out – and I'm sure that I have – then I can only apologise for the oversight. I remain grateful, nevertheless.

As always, I thank God for the life I have and count my blessings for everyone in it.

ABOUT THE AUTHOR

Paul Cuddihy is the author of the 'Costello Trilogy' novels – Saints and Sinners (2010), The Hunted (2011), Land Beyond The Wave (2012). He also wrote the best-selling biography, Tommy Burns: A Supporter Who Got Lucky (2009) and co-wrote Century Bhoys: A History of Celtic's Greatest Goalscorers (2010).

Made in the USA
Charleston, SC
03 March 2014